Tales of a
SOUTHERN
PALAZZO

Tales of a SOUTHERN PALAZZO

A Memoir

JOHN CLARK MCCALL, JR.

Outskirts Press, Inc.
Denver, Colorado

Outskirts Press, Inc.
http://www.outskirtspress.com

ISBN: 978-1-4327-7199-7

Outskirts Press and the "OP" logo are trademarks belonging to Outskirts Press, Inc.

PRINTED IN THE UNITED STATES OF AMERICA

For Mitch

Introduction: Violets, Vodka, and Vigoro ®

YOU HAVE TO understand that I come from a land where one could not contemplate existence without boiled peanuts. The list continues… salted toasted pecans, cheese straws (preferably Mimi Platter's), country ham, collard and turnip greens, REAL cornbread (not that sweet Yankee stuff)—and to leave the culinary list momentarily (only *momentarily*), crown mouldings, functional shutters, the summer's roses and zinnias, George Shearing, Ella Fitzgerald, Nat King Cole, and of course, *Frank*. Which brings us to the problem of securing a title for this exercise.

It has been a formidable task to put pen to paper for this book that I *have* to write. I promised myself that if I could ever find a suitable title, I would begin the project, which is simple enough in structure—retelling my own story of growing up in South Georgia using a singularly unusual edifice in Moultrie, Georgia as the backdrop. More on the *Palazzo* later.

One hurried day in readying for a party (My Aunt Alyce always pronounced it "paaaty" so you knew it was going to be special.), I looked at my shopping list and there, in a beautiful composition of innocent alliteration, sang out my first three items…

Violets, Vodka, and Vi-go-ro®. That trio of must-haves says a great deal about me, my world, and my friends. But, somehow, this title just didn't encapsulate the overall tale I had to tell. I stalled further because I introduced a new codicil to the agreement—I would also have to come up with the very first lines. Eating the last of summer's boiled peanuts from Allegood's (Moultrie's celebrated answer to the country delicatessen) did it. They are frozen, no less, but the fragrance of summer still surfaces as they defrost, leading me to "do something constructive and apply myself" (as my mother, Carolyn, often preached) and begin this journey. To limit myself in some way and to curb my natural A.D.D. tendencies, I've attempted to restrict my verbiage to the confines of a singularly distinctive mansion that cements all of the Southern waywardness I've conjured up, together with a bit of annotation on the characters (and I do mean *characters*) that are as much a part of its fabric as the stone urns which adorn the entablature. So here unfold the outlandish—but true—*Tales of a Southern Palazzo*.

Contents

My brother, William Frank McCall, III fly casting.
Collection of the Author

CHAPTER 1

Spanish Moss

I MUST WARN you that a shopping list enumerating violets, vodka, and fertilizer may sound innocent enough to our new millennium minds, but as we make this journey you will see just how complex, twisted, and highly fragrant a story wrapped in Spanish Moss can be. You guessed it, Spanish Moss is only a light disguise for the *people* of my world.

I quite innocently thought that most folks were just like my family, and since my mother and father both enjoyed three and four siblings respectively, that extended unit served as a great vessel for navigating my early years of growing up in the South. And, as Southern tradition dictates, there were other "relatives" who, despite no links by blood, were just as much a part of the family table as *my* only sibling, Willie (William Frank McCall, III).

One of these "relatives" was Robert Byrd Wright, Jr., or *Brother.* This Southern *Palazzo* which becomes the archive for the true stories I have to tell was conceived by Brother (he gained the name "Brother" because his childhood was inseparable from the comings and goings of my father, John Clark McCall, Sr. and my uncles, Sherrod Garland McCall, Sr., and William Frank McCall, Jr., at the McCall and Wright homes on Moultrie's *Southern Terrace*. This latter gentleman, Uncle Frank, a talented architect, designer, and later a Fellow of the American Institute of Architects brought the *Palazzo* to fruition.

Brother was the quintessential Southern bachelor, duly living in style with his mother, Bernice, and embodying what I thought to be the essence of what a renaissance man should look like, talk like, dress like; well, right down to the car, the antiques, and…the *house*. Brother Wright was one of four children born to Robert Byrd Wright, Sr., who made a comfortable fortune in the Ford car business, selling Model T's and A's to farmers in Colquitt County—Georgia's most fertile agricultural region. Mr. and Mrs. Wright were God-fearing Methodists and became very close to my paternal grandparents, Mr. and Mrs. William Francis McCall. They were collectively very sober and sensible people, but when one looks at the simple arithmetic of having four or five children, at least in the South, a minimum of one is going to turn out to be a little different, or *colorful*, as my Aunt Alyce used to put it.

The gestation of these "colorful" men in South Georgia seems to follow a pattern, and one that I find to hold true for myself: enjoying a fairly normal childhood, doing the expected, prescribed things—but picking fairy lilies by the road side, developing an early interest in *objects artsy*, playing with girls when we are supposed to be playing with boys, growing up, choosing not to marry, living with our mothers, and attempting to confront our sexual differences in a region of the country that sweeps those differences right up with helping mother in the kitchen and setting the table with the best Minton china and Tiffany flatware. Colorful men have all learned the painful lesson that we can find acceptance in our lifestyle as long as Mama is not confronted face-to-face with the fact that there are NOT going to be any grandchildren in our future and the man that becomes our "best friend" might just be sharing our finest monogrammed percale!

My father, who possessed a true gift for writing could have, perhaps, done a much better job with this saga but his affair with the bottle got in the way, and when that wasn't the issue, his passion for game hunting literally possessed him, squashing the F. Scott Fitzgerald and the Thomas Wolfe that most assuredly lived within. I know my father was also very much aware that Uncle Frank and Brother Wright were delightfully different, and it never seemed to be an issue for him (or was it?). In any event, the reader (especially my Northern friends) must accept the premise—before we march on—that every Southern town has its colorful men. They are as much a part of the community as the

Colonial Revival funeral home, a Homecoming Church Revival (beware of ministers of music though married with children!), or the house in the style of the Greek Revival (or Greek *Survival*, as my friend Berrien Cheatham catalogues it). By the way, Berrien describes himself—at least after a scotch or two—as a *retired homosexual*. His marvelous wit and his facility with malapropisms will surface throughout this book.

In 1960 my father was released from Tri-State Tractor Co. John had been an effective sales representative (I still remember evenings when he would call from Vidalia, Georgia where I was born, to Albany (not New York), giving the operator Tri-State's number which always began as "Hemlock Five…"). I was given a bright yellow model of a Caterpillar motor-grader but I had much rather have had some records or stamps for my album (he should have known something was afoot!). My Daddy's frequent visits with *Jim Beam* finally took their toll, Tri-State fired him, and in the summer of 1960, we packed up and moved to Moultrie—a town where both of my parents grew up.

I recall the moving day well, as Daddy had "tied one on" and gave Carolyn unmitigated hell about transporting some pot plants—that couldn't go in the moving van—in the comfort and safety of our 1957 Oldsmobile Eighty-Eight sedan. Our maid, Jay, had made her famous date tarts for the last time and Carolyn let Willie and me comfort ourselves with those delectable confections as we made our way to Moultrie. Moultrie had always been a second home, so I looked upon the move as something rather exciting despite the fact that our "new" residence was a rather dilapidated World War II tract house. The washing machine overflowed into the floor furnace the very night we moved in. We had enjoyed central air in our modern duplex in Vidalia and Carolyn had gone to Rich's in Atlanta and purchased some wonderful furniture—all of which we still have and enjoy today. She did her best in the house on Fourteenth Street in Moultrie, probably crying under her pillow many nights—but never letting us know. Moultrie served as our new home mainly because my grandmother, Susie Clark McCall had given Daddy a job at the family farm. We picked eggplant and trucked them to Cagle's Grocery to sell. We even wrapped them in thin tissue like some sort of below-the-Mason-Dixon-Line *Harry and David*!

Moultrie was a larger town than Vidalia, Georgia (I always judged towns by the size of their theatres and Moultrie's newly-remodeled Colquitt was just immense to me in contrast to Vidalia's Pal). I already knew "Mr. Brother" from our many visits to the seat of Colquitt County. He was always kind and really interested in what was going on with my family—and particularly with me. He went bird hunting with Daddy. I think he spotted my artistic side readily (I can't imagine why sketching interiors of French furniture, listening to theatre organ records, painting watercolors, and being involved in musicals would give him such clues!).

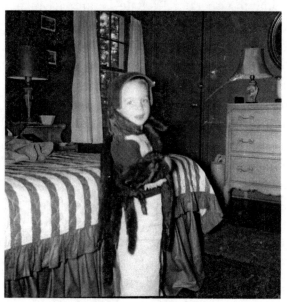

Me in "early drag", Vidalia, GA.
Collection of the Author

Now, mind you, this interest was always an innocent one and that interest never crossed the line, *ever*. When Brother needed a little "color" he left Moultrie on business trips or personal travel that probably afforded the amenities and privacy that bigger cities like Atlanta had to offer. I suspect that some of his exotic travel in later years to the Caribbean may have spelled the tragic end of his life. I'm pretty certain that he might have fallen victim to an early case of "the plague"—so early that doctors at Emory Hospital had no clue what was going on in his poor, emaciated body.

Brother and me at the Beach Club Pool, Sea Island, Summer, 1954.
Collection of the Author

But let's return to the Camelot of 1960 where Brother became a regular fixture in our family—in addition to the longstanding association he had with Uncle Frank and my Uncle Sherrod and Aunt Alyce. This *Palazzo* business all started one Sunday when Brother drove his sister-in-law's big black 1960 Continental Mark V onto our driveway (I swear that car extended from the street entrance to our front door step!). He announced that he had purchased the Paramount Theatre Building or, so I thought) in Atlanta and had engaged Uncle Frank to design a new villa of the Palladian order for his lot on Tallokas Road (Berrien Cheatham would prophetically re-name this street *Alice B. Toklas Road*). I already knew of this fine edifice from Ben Hall's book on the golden age of the movie palace, *The Best Remaining Seats* and I was also aware that it still had its three-manual Wurlitzer theatre organ. When I queried Brother about buying the theatre's contents, he clarified his former statement by letting me know that he had only purchased the theatre's façade and some bronze announcement frames. I pouted for weeks because I really thought that Brother was the richest man I knew—and I wanted that organ (where in the hell would I have put it?).

The Atlanta Paramount Theatre, Peachtree Street, c.1932.
Elliott's Studio

When the façade arrived in Moultrie on flatbed trucks, the lot on Tallokas suddenly became something akin to a stage set for a de Mille epic. There were cartouches and balusters, and pediments and quoins, and urns and columns, and pilasters…well, you get the picture. The most interesting Easter egg hunts of childhood memory were held there. And because Brother was so thick with Sherrod and Alyce, he lured them from their rambling Victorian house on our family farm to the "city" by offering them half of his lot. Alyce's daughter, Molly—my first cousin—and I mounted some of the greatest spectacles of Roman tragedy and comedy amidst those "ruins". The Paramount had been designed by the prestigious Atlanta firm of Hentz, Reid, and Adler. Originally named the Howard, the primary architect for this magnificent and classically correct building was Philip Trammell Shutze—a man that Uncle Frank held on an equally classically proportioned pedestal. Shutze was to later be honored by Classical America for his contributions to architectural classicism, and in 1986 Kitty Carlisle Hart handed Frank the same Arthur Ross Award.

Well, you can just imagine the commentary from the common folk as this marvelous structure began to take form just south of Allegood's Grocery and Alyce and Sherrod's Frank McCall vernacular farm house with its rocking chairs on a porch of old brick. A respected and venerable employee of Wright Motor Company remarked, "Yessuh, Mistuh Brother done bought hisself a picture show!" My Great Aunt Willie Maude ("Aunt Bill" she demanded to be called) after coming down from Tennille said, "Humphh—it looks like a post office to me!" Oh how the architecturally deprived can show their ignorance.

The *Palazzo*, c.1964.
Bowles Studio

Now, you have to remember that these days of Camelot were marked with a runaway hit on television, *The Beverly Hillbillies*. And there were indeed some similarities. For one, Brother's mother, Miss

Bernice, grew turnip greens under the imported I-talian cedars Brother had planted near the fountain in the rear courtyard. She sometimes sent some 'round and they were quite a delicacy. I can still see the tiny cracklin' corn breads which had been hand-formed with little ridges made by her cook's fingers, toasted to a golden brown on the top of the pot. The Wright's poodle was named Jacques, as in the TV series. Mimi Platter, another Moultrie *grande dame* once was invited to bring her poodle over to visit Jacques. Mimi lamented that "Reggie" would be the only member of the Platter family to ever be entertained at the *Palazzo* (this was a humorous fib). Although there was no "cement pond", one found a magnificent courtyard with an imported fountain that held goldfish in the top of its glassed-in lavabo. Oh, and there were gates—with marvelous coat of arms, and although there were no Imperials like Milburn Drysdale drove, there were Lincolns and Thunderbirds. The Imperials would come to 20 Tallokas Road much later, but then we are getting ahead of our story. Of course, we must remember that, despite Bernice's penchant for growing greens 'neath the cedars, the Wright household was much more *Drysdalian* than Clampett.

While we're discussing pedigree, I will never forget driving by Jim Williams' *Mercer House* (made famous in the book and film, *Midnight in the Garden of Good and Evil*) and having my passenger, Uncle Frank, exclaim in his Southern drawl (which sprang from an elixir combining the likes of Tennessee Williams and Truman Capote): "I'd jest give anything to be invited to *that* house and meet Jim Williams!" Well even at a tender young age, I knew this was the most preposterous thing I'd ever heard from WFM. Both Frank and Brother gained their sophistication through their birthright. Jim Williams manufactured his—albeit to a high degree. Jim Williams should have been clamoring to invite the likes of Uncle Frank and Brother, and in fact, later on he did.

Uncle Frank and Brother had a long-standing friendship that was tinged with a little competitiveness from time to time. Brother was sweepingly handsome: , tall, elegant, without a trace of effeminacy, and well-educated in the arts and architecture primarily through self study.

Brother and Dottie at a dinner party in Frank's Hillcrest Office, 1950's.
Collection of the Author

He was, like Jim Williams, a competent antiquarian as well. But Brother could sometimes pontificate and re-embroider the provenance of an item which would leave Frank in a caustic and sarcastic mood. Frank was portly, short, somewhat effeminate in his speech, but highly educated in the arts and architecture, guided by study at Auburn University and fueled by a passion and innate talent that touched everything he did. There was a natural flow to Frank's talents that let you know that he had it all safely tucked away in his little finger. He had no concept of being boastful and he rarely showed his jealousies—well, until the martinis flowed too fast and too often. Then, we really had a problem. Brother seemed to always consistently hold his liquor and maintain a façade—even if carefully manufactured—that left people somewhat breathless. Though the ownership of Wright Motor Company passed to him, he never really "sold" cars regularly; that was something for his salesmen.

Uncle Frank in the Solarium at *The Hedges*, Sea Island.
Collection of the Author

I saw first-hand the catty side of this relationship at Brother's one evening. He invited me over for a drink at the *Palazzo*—just us. Brother always genuinely wanted to know what was going on in MY life, so I was expounding on my doings in Atlanta when suddenly the phone rang. Brother and I were in the English Study at the fireplace and I couldn't have been four feet from my host when he handed me the phone. It was Uncle Frank, in his cups. In a highly-fueled tone of voice Frank said, "What are you doin'?" I replied, "Brother and I are just catching up on what's been goin' on." Frank, almost interrupting said, "He's gonna ask you to go upstahusz and see the new gall'ry we jest completed for him and he's gonna show you the new Degas. It's a FAKE!" I know Brother heard all this, but I simply said, "Well it's so good of you to call; I'll give Brother your regards." And I put down the phone. I learned after that—firsthand—there were eggshells lying around when I talked about Uncle Frank and Brother Wright in the same breath. I'm surprised that Frank didn't throw up the fact that Miss Bernice's name and not Brother's was on the blueprints for the *Palazzo*!

Aunt Alyce in the Library of *Iris Court.*
Collection of the Author

CHAPTER 2

"Big A"

IF BROTHER AND Uncle Frank were clumps of Spanish Moss, then Aunt Alyce was the Crape Myrtle to which they and all the other little mosslets clung. Alyce NeSmith McCall is really the *roux* that holds this story together. I don't know why in God's name I have withheld painting her persona until now. I guess it's because you need a good perspective on Brother and Frank to truly appreciate Alyce. Though some of her personality was carefully processed, it always "came off", and to the uninitiated, they couldn't figure out what had hit them. People were just downright in awe of Alyce—or "Big A" as her dearest friends called her. I would not describe Alyce as beautiful but—handsome—my yes! She was always impeccably groomed, singularly striking in exquisitely tailored clothes, with just the right adornment from a copious jewelry box much owed to the generosity of Uncle Frank and Juan—a character I have yet to introduce. Now, that's the "paaaty" description. But Alyce had an earthiness—imported from her birthplace of Pelham, Georgia—that could find her at home in the most utilitarian costume while she refinished a piece of furniture from the antique shop in Pavo, tended her roses, or churned home-made spearmint ice cream on the back porch. She was also the most gifted improviser of story-telling that I ever knew. No story ever came out the same twice—it took on a delivery appropriate for the audience at hand—and always, there was a perfect punch line causing people to pound the floor. She actually looked very much like Queen Elizabeth II, but she had a much better sense of humor and she was slightly less regal. Alyce met my uncle, Sherrod Garland McCall (why couldn't I have had that prized middle name?—I'm colorful!) during World War II while she was serving as an able secretary to Moultrie mogul, William J. Vereen of Riverside Manufacturing Company.

My Uncle Sherrod was just about the handsomest thing in all of Colquitt County—next to my father, of course, who resembled Jason Robards. And Alyce and Sherrod became quite a social machine after their marriage and the adoption of my two cousins, Molly and Sherrod, Jr. Uncle Sherrod joined Harper-McCall Insurance (where my grandfather was a partner after he closed his grocery business) upon returning home from his tour in the Pacific. They settled in on the Clark-McCall farm I mentioned earlier in a rambling Victorian farmhouse.

Me with my father and Lana Turner—I mean *Carolyn*!
Little's Studio

When we came to visit from Vidalia, "The Farm" was just about the greatest thing I knew. I got to ride "Brownie", a fine pony, and later "Joker", a half-crazy horse who owned up to his name. Molly and I bathed together in the old claw-foot cast iron tub. I can still see the Ivory soap floating, courtesy of Alyce's filling up the Ford Country Wagon at Rich Oil Company in town. Alyce was a grand cook, and she was even better at getting "the help" to prepare memorable meals of fried chicken, scalloped oysters, rice and gravy, and tiny biscuit. We always had Mayhaw jelly with those biscuit and I grew up thinking this was something you could buy off any food market shelf. Now, I know better about this little berry that is indigenous to the bogs of Southwest Georgia!

The grown-ups must have had just as much fun at the farm—or maybe more. Alyce knew how to entertain and Sherrod saw to it that there was always a fully stocked bar. Alyce had the recipe for a party down pat, just as if it was for a making of deviled eggs.

First off, the most precocious Johnny and Molly were sent to the playhouse in back where Molly had a fully-optioned Easy-Bake Oven. Now Alyce knew that an oven powered by a solitary light bulb could make cooking a hen egg an all-day culinary affair. So we tended the egg while the adults partied away. By the time the egg was cooked, so were the McCall's and their friends, and we carefully made our entrance to the front grand parlor somewhat like Tootie's entrance in the film, *Meet Me in St. Louis*. We were the adored duo who did our version of the "fanny dance"—our derrieres back-to-back while the hit song *Fanny* played on the RCA Victor. We knew how to market an exhibition that promised little art or grace—it was, rather, all a matter of perfect timing. In fact, we upstaged the Dave Gardner recordings that had been playing prior to our most theatrical of entrances.

By the time we were permanent residents in Moultrie in 1960, Alyce and Sherrod were firmly planted on one end of Brother's lot. And from that station, Alyce forever controlled the neighborhood—even the *Palazzo* that was to rise beyond her kitchen window. Brother and Alyce had a special relationship and when he had just about enough of his "la-de-da" guests and parties, Alyce's heart pine kitchen table spelled relief and a homecoming to the more agrarian side of Moultrie and environs. Brother actually never lost his small town side either; that's one reason he clicked so well with the Sherrod McCall's. He was a master at keeping his earthier visage hidden if need be, but he was still a small town boy, with a grand, well-balanced sense of humor.

Alyce could find humor everywhere; she didn't just have to manufacture it. In later years she'd type me letters as if she were at the old *Royal* at Riverside and enclose some of the most priceless newspaper clippings you've ever read. Often, they were from the *Pelham Journal*. One clipping that has stayed with me over the years is the wedding write-up that went to great lengths to describe the brand of cologne that the groomsmen wore. Alyce and Sherrod were always in the center of Moultrie's social whirlpool, and they were very open to all kinds of folk—but especially those who might lead them up another rung or bring profit to Harper-McCall. This included the "colorful" social component as well. They were well aware of Uncle Frank's persuasion which he tried to hide while "locked in a closet" whose key was alcohol. In fact, I think the *key* was Frank's crutch for his sexual dilemma. And Sherrod and Alyce were open and immensely tolerant of Brother and even several gay *couples*, which was something of an anomaly back then. Brother once tried to have a relationship right under everybody's nose, but it was with an assistant Methodist minister with a wife and children; Alyce and Sherrod remained tolerant and patient, but the partnership ended in disaster.

At some point, Alyce's relationship with Brother went awry, but only after his gift of a beautiful Chinese lacquered cabinet that graced her attractive living room. I don't think that it had a thing to do with persuasion, or "color"; quite possibly, it may have been business or some problem with her steadfast relationship with Dorothy Ogden Wright, Brother's wealthy sister-in-law who lived in a large McCall-designed home on Granada Boulevard in Coral Gables, Florida. For years rumor had it that The Beatles stayed there on their first trip to the United States after flying in to nearby Miami to begin their first U.S. concert tour in February, 1964. They actually stayed with Dorothy's sister, Betty Ogden Garvey on Miami's Star Island. *They were smuggled over in a laundry truck to escape Beatle-crazed fans.*

Portrait of Dottie.
Collection of the Author

Alyce had her own language and it was a by-product of her astute ability to listen, appreciate, and synthesize the best that Southern humanity had to offer. This included our black friends, or I should say *family*. Alyce and Sherrod were particularly good to anyone in their employ and they actually tended to one family financially for decades.

In later years Alyce and Sherrod groomed Greg Richardson as a butler and a mighty fine one was he. In his white coat he served everything from mint juleps and sausage pinwheels to iced tea and hot yeast rolls, always with a grace that could have placed him squarely in the Oak Room at the Plaza. I once asked Alyce how Greg was working out and she replied (Brace yourself, for she meant this totally in jest.) "Fine… honey, I wished I owned me three mo of 'em!" She'd keep a straight face after that charged retort, but you knew that she was dying from laughter inside. To Greg, his charge was like being in some Southern drama. He played "the game"…and laughed all the way to the bank. Actually Alyce and Sherrod were supportive of Moultrie's unusually small Black community and working for the Sherrod McCall's meant employment with many extra benefits—never servitude!

The Aristocrats: Del and Greg Richardson.
Collection of the Author

Through the years since the building of the *Palazzo*, Alyce had to ingratiate, manipulate, and tolerate (in that order of ownership) three polychromed bachelor residents. Her dilemma is really the axis on which *Tales of a Southern Palazzo* spins, where Alyce rules as the one and only *prima donna*—even beyond the grave. The remarkable thing about all this is that these stories are true. I may have embroidered them with a little extra thread for color and contrast, but essentially and in the spirit of our Southern code, they are quite real. Let's see if we can astound you in the successive chapters.

CHAPTER **3**

The Big Paaaty, Part One

IT CAN BE emphatically established that the City of Moultrie is one hell of a dichotomous spot in South Georgia. On one side there is a populace strewn among the fields of the state's most fertile agricultural region—families with meager incomes and little education and lots of religion. Then, in the midst of all this, you find quite the opposite: the Pidcock's, the Vereen's, the Friedlander's, the Kirk's, the Platter's, of course, the Wright's, and the wanna-be McCall's, just to name a few. The McCall's never really had the money of the aforementioned but they spent a lot of time—with Frank as the high priest—in convincing you that they did. Frank probably reached his pinnacle when he was invited to become a member of Atlanta's Piedmont Driving Club.

It is with particular pleasure (and pride) that I offer one of the few extant pieces my father wrote outside of his sports column for *The Moultrie Observer*. To me, and to many of my kin and kith, it captures the essence of small-town Moultrie—a domain of the hard-working, God-fearing common man. It provides a striking contrast to the elite of Tallokas Road and environs and, to this day, such a contrast still pervades Colquitt County. John Sr. wrote this as a young man, observing Moultrie's bustling downtown fabric on a Saturday in the late thirties. His observation point was probably McCall's Grocery on First Street; William Francis McCall (my grandfather), proprietor...

They Come To Town Each Saturday

They come to town each Saturday
Like doves to a baited field.
They come just like they are
For they have nothing to conceal.

Some come in wagons drawn by mules,
Some come in Model T's;
Some come in new cars—fenders bent,
And driving where they please.

They sit and stand around the square
And roll their cigarettes;
And hem and haw about the drought
And fertilizer debts.

They enter any grocery store
And call for black-eyed peas.
They say they want a bubble gum
And some of them thar cheese.

They say they want some "resins", too.
These folk, they need no manners.
They say they want a big red drink
To eat with they b-nanners.

I like to sit and watch them pass—
The boys and girls, I mean.
And it would make a bloodhound smile
To see the sights I've seen.

And when the Georgia sun is gone,
They—riding arm-in-arm,
Leave their trash to the fading town
And head back to the farm.

Leaving Moultrie's courthouse square, and traveling under two miles, one found quite another world at 20 Tallokas Road on Saturday evening, June 1, 1963. Of course, I did not get to attend the party, and I did not even grandstand at the side fence like the Beard and Meadors children did while their parents danced away at certainly the biggest private social event to ever unfold in the city. Fortunately, Yolande Gwin, *The Atlanta Journal's* society editor offered a charming recount of the event with pictures of the guests that could have been posed by Fabian Bachrach himself.

The entrance steps were covered in a red runner and a specially constructed dance floor had been built over the rear courtyard to accommodate Albert Murphy and his Orchestra. The terpsichorean exhibitions of Brother's guests must have been something as everyone whirled the night away and chatted with Georgia Governor Carl Sanders and his wife, Betty Foy. As Laura Beard—who had her own Uncle Frank house on *Alice B. Toklas*—remarked to Miss Gwin, "If I had Elizabeth Taylor and Richard Burton on my front porch across the street right now, nobody would even glance at them." Uncle Frank was reported as bringing in an "elaborate arrangement" for the dining room as he ascended the carpeted entrance. No one will ever know for sure how Frank felt about his masterpiece, or to the degree that Brother claimed credit for what had materialized, but it is certain that Frank drank a good deal at the party and had to be "taken home" where he was put to bed by my grandmother, "Nanny." I often witnessed those "putting Frank to bed" episodes where an inebriated Frank would go into his torch song: *You Made Me Love You.* It was dramatic enough, but Frank, like most of the McCall's, couldn't carry a tune in a bucket. My grandmother would dutifully get Frank undressed, install his Brooks Brothers pajamas (adorned with a "WFM" diamond monogram) and say in her wee but firm voice, "Now Frank, I'm not going to have this; get in this bed". That's when Frank would go into his reprise—with more power and less musicality than ever. Frank was a Garland lover—like all good refined men of his era—and I often wonder if he was singing this to his "Gable", for the pain and drama were readily there to let one know it was all about unrequited love.

My father, who would rather be sipping his bubbly in a duck blind, did take my mother Carolyn to the party. And I am most certain that he ascribed to the McCall heritage of taking in too much. He may have been a "happy" drunk that night (and I do hope so, because his other side was not appealing). If he was in a less antagonistic mood, he might have even recited this poem to some guest who would give him the time:

A She-up and A Go-it

(He would always announce the title—hands by his side—as if he were in a grammar school convocation.)

> A she-up and a go-it
> They was walkin' in the pasture.
>
> Said the she-up to the go-it,
> "Can't you walk a little faster?"
>
> Said the go-it to the she-up,
> "My foot are sore."
>
> Said the she-up to the go-it,
> "Excuse me, go-it;
> I didn't know it."

Now, Daddy would get right in your face to do this delivery and he was so affected and on-stage that you had to laugh, even if it wasn't real funny. My former partner and mentor, Glenn Thomas once made an astute observation about my mother and father. He said, "The only problem with John and Carolyn is that they each want to be in the spotlight...alone." While my mother mambos and Charlestons her way through this party (not with John, who wasn't a dancer), I guess I should give the reader a brief portrait of Moultrie's answer to Auntie Mame. Well, that actually sums it up.

CHAPTER 4

About Carolyn Kay McCall

CAROLYN WAS THE eldest of the lovely Kay sisters, followed by my Aunt Martha and the youngest of the three, Aunt Mary Frances. The Kay sisters were blessed with a fine brother, Billy Kay, who was the youngest of all. The Kay sisters—in their youth—lived in Moultrie longer than

Carolyn trips the light fantastic with a Cloister dance instructor, c. 1956.
Sea Island Co.

The Hatfields and The McCoy's: "Big A" with my Aunt Martha Kay Thomas.
Collection of the Author

any other city. My grandfather, Wallace Kay, was a rather peripatetic linotype operator. During the Kay family's Moultrie era, my mother and my aunts dated almost every male Moultrian named in this book, and they all took turns with Brother Wright.

Carolyn really should have married a wealthy man, and when Daddy would go on week-long tears, I'd sincerely ask Carolyn why she couldn't marry Brother (I had no clue back then that he wasn't the marrying type. Brother had me fooled along with the multitudes.) Carolyn began to take on affectations that would make you truly believe she was some sort of movie star…and she managed somehow to have the clothes and the *shoes* to convince you. I well remember many times, usually in a car, that Daddy would glance over at Carolyn and say, "Carolyn, isn't that a new outfit?" And Carolyn would respond, "Oh, it's just something I picked up." **"Picked Up**?" Daddy would exclaim. **"PICKED UP**?!" Carolyn, in trying to lessen the blow, just made it all the worse. Daddy would get red in the face, then it would all be dropped and we would motor on just as if nothing had happened.

Another in-transit episode was when we were making our way from Vidalia to Moultrie and Daddy had stopped to get Carolyn some potato chips. Carolyn got very quiet and just kind of played with the bag as we approached a stop sign coming in to Tifton. Daddy looked over at Carolyn and said, "Is something wrong?" Carolyn, in the most nonchalant voice she could muster said, "Oh, no..." "What is it, Carolyn!" he retorted. And in the most diminutive voice you've ever heard she replied, "You didn't get *Tom's*." Daddy reached over, not minding the road, and snatched the chips out of her hands and tossed them onto the pavement of Highway 125. At first things got very quiet, then Carolyn cracked up, followed by Willie and me, and Daddy finally gained control of the road again. We stopped at the *Alpine* restaurant in Tifton and had a good meal, prior to making our grand entrance into Moultrie.

Carolyn had unerring taste in everything and she could charm everyone from Vestal Goodman, who once broke the Ten Commandments and openly coveted Carolyn's mink coat as we strolled through a mall in Charlotte, to Armand Hammer, who dined at Brother Wright's and was served by Carolyn—replete with a French Maid's uniform. She loved to cultivate new partygoers, and would often bring John by the sleeve to "meet these *lovely* new people." "Uh, now, what was your name?" she'd ask. Her friend, Ida Murphy had a remedy for that awkward situation. She always suggested that, if the name had evaporated, one should simply say, "Honey, come ovah heah 'n meet Sugah."

Even after I became very sure about who I was, Carolyn still hoped that I would somehow miraculously change and give her some grandchildren that she could treat like Patrick Dennis—right down to red leather bedroom shoes from Best & Company in New York. My mother's two sisters—both of whom were much better off materially than Carolyn but who had their Capezios a little more on the ground— often said, "We don't know *where* Carolyn came from!"

She was pretty hard on me and unfailingly easy on my brother Willie. But she loved me "good" as Alyce used to say, and I gave her back the same. Her Hollywood mystique was never more evident than when she rode out with Daddy to pay a call on a family who were rather poor sharecroppers. They had the obligatory ringer washer and old sofa on the front porch, and the chickens beneath. I'm sure Carolyn had on one of her latest Chanel suits and some tortoise shell sunglasses and maybe one of the pins Frank gave her from Charles Willis or Tiffany. She, of course, stayed in the car while Daddy talked to Leo about an upcoming dove shoot (Leo was Daddy's bird caddy). Well, the children just couldn't get over Carolyn, and the mother of some of them, Maxie (who was later to be a live-in caretaker for Bernice Wright) issued an invitation for Carolyn to join them at a birthday party for one of the children complete with a *home-made* birthday cake and ice cream. The *home-made* part got to Carolyn right away and she emphatically told John that she just could not stomach food in such an unkempt place. For once, Daddy had the upper hand, and he told her in no uncertain terms that she *would* go and she *would* eat cake and ice cream. Carolyn obliged, and the afternoon gave her a bit of true and tender reality. The children made over her so, you would have thought she was Shirley McLaine. The experience put a big lump in her throat and when she returned to the city, she began packing some much-needed clothing items for the children which Daddy dutifully delivered. Weeks later, Carolyn was shopping for capers and caviar in the local Winn-Dixie, when a good friend greeted her in the aisle. She said, "Carolyn, I tell you, nobody on earth hunts birds with more class than John." Carolyn asked, "Pray tell, explain." "Well," the friend mused, "there's John tramping over the field with the South Georgia sun setting behind him, followed by Leo picking up doves and putting them in a Neiman-Marcus shopping bag."

When my Great Uncle Lamar Brantley from Tennille died, all the Kay's had assembled in Billy and Mary Grace Kay's family room prior to the processional for the funeral. We were having a good time and I believe there were some Bloody Mary's or something of the sort to render reinforcement. I had given Carolyn my jazzy Oldsmobile Cutlass when I traded cars. I had specially-ordered it and it fit her to a "T". Well, my Aunt Mary Frances, who could have owned ten Cutlasses if she had wished, had a similar one with a standard blue velour interior. The funeral director made his way around the jolly group to inquire about whose car was whose so that the processional could be initiated. He got to Mary Frances and she said, quite simply, "I have the blue Cutlass". He inventoried a few more and then got to Carolyn. Carolyn put down her bloody and announced, "Mine's the beige Cutlass, with the *red leather interior.*"

Now, please know that the saving grace of Carolyn was that she could laugh first and hardest about her airs and her a-little-bit-better countenance. I've never seen her laugh more heartily than when I was serving as a Junior Host at the posh Cloister Hotel on Sea Island, Georgia. "C-Island"—as the McCall's drawled it out, was our watering hole for every summer I can ever remember. We couldn't afford to go in "the season" and Frank had to recruit practically everybody in the family—including some cousins once removed—to get enough money up to rent a "cottage" for two weeks each summer.

Carolyn gives a *bow* to *Clara Bow* at *The Hedges*, Summer, 1987.
Collection of the Author

When I became employed at Sea Island through the support of my dear friend and fellow Moultrian, Cloister Social Director Laura Dunn (our answer to Tallulah Bankhead), you would have thought Carolyn saw me as the new Speaker of the House or something. On one of my off nights, not having to cater to rich Yankee spinsters and bratty South Georgia millionaire children, I invited Carolyn to join me in the clubrooms for drinks and dancing. Well, that was like St. Peter sending her on up to the pen-ultimate penthouse at the Waldorf. She was beautifully attired, I was be-tuxed, and while Daddy hunted and drank and sometimes worked back in Moultrie, we danced the night away. When we entered the clubrooms, the orchestra struck up *Alley Cat* which was Carolyn's sainted Sea Island hymn tune.

Laura Dunn and me at the *Beach Club*, summer, 1969.
Sea Island Co.

The Cloister Hotel's porte cochere was a world famous, and often-photographed feature of society architect Addison Mizner's original 1928 Mediterranean masterpiece. I was delighted that I had my 1963 Lincoln Continental valet-parked for the evening. The Continental was a luscious turquoise with matching turquoise leather—of course—and brocade. But I had bought it used—I guess very used—and it had been lovely to look at and a bitch to keep on the road. Well, there we were, stationed on the top step under the porte cochere when the lovely Lincoln made its entrance. Just as the valet opened the car door, there was a sudden hiss under the hood and a cloud of steam emerged that could have given the *Ile de France* a run for its money. I left Carolyn at the top step while she tried to find a convenient hibiscus bush under which to hide. I couldn't get the car to start for love or money. Everything on that Lincoln, of course, was backward. The hood was hinged at the front and the four doors were of the infamous "suicide" variety. Why couldn't we have just been in a Simca or something? I finally had to get the valet to help me push the foundering sedan out into the parking lot. I sold that Lincoln to one of the Hotel's kitchen help, or rather, I practically gave it to her.

Earlier that same summer, the Lincoln had caused another stir and Aunt Alyce could tell this one like no other. I had been having radiator problems and the car was staying more at the Brunswick Lincoln-Mercury dealer than at the Sea Island employee barracks where I lived in my summer position. I was out of money and needed to get the radiator re-cored, so I thought I would pop over to Cottage 40 where Carolyn and Aunt Alyce were *ensconced* (Daddy loved that rather phony word). I didn't know that the night previous, Carolyn and Alyce had "done the clubrooms" and done 'em right. Carolyn probably had on some Bruno Magi's that she just had to have even though they weren't her size, and both of them danced and cocktailed into the wee hours until *Alley Cat* was put to sleep for good. Alyce must have been the better custodian; at least she was dressed and awake the morning after. I kind of burst onto the front glassed-in porch and asked, "Where's Carolyn?" (I gave up the "mother" thing years ago; you can't dance the night away in the clubrooms with *Mother*; that could only be done on the *Lawrence*

Welk Show!) Alyce had a very stern look on her face; she was walking in a labored sort of way as she got right at eye level and said, "I don't think you'd better be callin' Carolyn right now, Johnny. Yo mutha's in the bed and she isn't feelin' too good." "I need to see her right now!" I demanded, and I made my way up the steps. It was morbidly quiet up there and Alyce was stationed—stone-faced—at the bottom of the balustrade. I knocked on the door. "Carolyn, I've got to talk to you about the Lincoln; I need to borrow some money to get the..." **BAM!** From out of nowhere appeared this apparition that looked like the Golden Coast's answer to Jacob Marley. Carolyn was bandaged up from head to foot and she stretched out her arms as if she was ready for the kill, screaming "Get out of this house before I murder youuuuu!" I ran like a jack rabbit. Alyce didn't say another word. Every time Alyce would tell this yarn, the part needed on the Lincoln would change; it might be a tire, or a battery. But one thing is for sure, on that very day of the chase, I learned to take more stock in Alyce's recommendations and her wisdom 'bout paaaty's and paaaty'in.

CHAPTER 5

More On "C-Island"

BEFORE I LET "C-Island" go, I have some more stories that have to fit somewhere in this rambling diatribe. Keep in mind that *Brown's Guide to Georgia* once published an article about the "South Georgia Crackers" going down to "The Island" for their much cherished day in the sun. Rates in the summer for cottage rentals were much more reasonable and it allowed those, like the McCall's, to hob-knob with the better families in the state and an occasional Yankee who had the poor judgment to stay behind and endure all that foolishness. Sea Island was, for Frank, a way to have an endless number of cocktail parties with Carolyn and Alyce (and a battery of maids) doing all the work. But *Brown's Guide* really hit the mark and I think the McCall family became "Exhibit A". It told of buying new uniforms for the help, shelling peas, and loading down the station wagons with items like rafts and liquor and the obligatory home-made cheese straws, Pepperidge Farm thin-sliced bread, and toasted pecans. Frank was incensed.

This brand of fun at the Island ended after Frank became professionally successful enough to raise his own cottage at Sea Island. On July 4, 1976, he dedicated *The Hedges*. Carolyn and John rode with him down from Moultrie for the gala event; Frank had to ask Daddy for the thirty-five cents to get over the toll bridge on the St. Simons Causeway. This elegant Regency home—with an opulent drawing room on the second floor—was one of Frank's masterpieces, but it demanded a new way of vacationing at Sea Island, and paaaty's became forever changed. Bill

Blass might have been a guest there, but it was just not the same.

But while the McCall's continued to descend on Cottage 40—pre-*Hedges*—those stucco walls could speak volumes about hilarious happenings. One of the stories I offer pre-dates my summer employment there: in 1968 as a waiter in the hotel, and in 1969 as the Junior Host of the social staff (talk about crossing the tracks!).

My Aunt Susan, one of the two McCall girls, was our most elegant McCall. After marrying George Patterson (mentioned in *Midnight in the Garden of Good and Evil*), she had a taste of the Palm Beach way of doing things as George was a bank president there. She even served scrambled eggs on a sterling silver tray! It was her turn to be at "The Island" and the Sherrod and John McCall's were booked at Cottage 40 for other weeks that summer. Their occupation was somewhat different than Aunt Susan's, so I very carefully planned my ensemble when I was asked to come down and visit for the weekend.

My first car was a 1949 Lincoln Cosmopolitan which my father purchased for me for $150.00. With 32,000 original miles the car was like unto the *S.S. Leviathan* but exceedingly dependable. It had, however, blemishes all around the bottom sheet metal as old Widow Stewart, a pillar of our Moultrie First Methodist Church, couldn't even see over the steering wheel, much less onto the various curbs of our municipality. I think her little hats were framed right between the top of the wheel and the horn button.

I knew how to blackmail my Daddy when he had been on an extraordinary "tear". After a few days of sobriety, I convinced him that my Lincoln should go to "Fussy" Blanton's body shop and get cosmetics. Daddy—who likened that to overhauling one of his fine L.C. Smith or Parker shotguns—couldn't do anything but oblige. Finally, the Lincoln looked stunning and I thought to myself, "Well I might not be going to Sea Island in a new Continental, but this old Cosmo will be perfectly suitable." (Oh, if I just had it now!).

McCall's do not go on trips without, what my Daddy used to enumerate, a pot plant, a freshly-iced cake, and a baby. Well, I didn't have the baby, but my grandmother Nanny made sure that I took a small Areca Palm and a lovely cocoanut cake to Aunt Susan.

It was mid-summer, I had the car spotlessly washed, and I packed all the accoutrements together with my carefully selected wardrobe of Brooks Brothers ties, madras shirts, and Gray Flannel cologne. I was making my way past Waycross on to Nahunta and stopped for gas. Back then, there was no "self-serve" and I had the Lincoln's oil and water checked, asked them to "fill 'er up and 'fluff' the tires", and I was back on the road. Suddenly, a huge "Trailaways" bus (that's how our black brethren said it) passed me and woosh!—up went the hood which had not been secured previously—over the windshield—and the Cosmo plummeted into a ravine of bulrushes and flycatchers. Splat went the cake and sploosh went the potted palm; I was just beside myself. In addition to all of this trauma, I had to drive the car with my head stuck outside the windshield in harm's way on the miniscule two-lane highway. I finally found a repair shop and they executed the hood's decapitation, handing me a bill and the hood ornament, which must have weighed in at seven pounds. I had to do my best to clean up the outrageous combination of Perlite, potting soil, yellow cake, and gooey cocoanut icing that had somehow become one horrendous, homogenous mass.

I was demoralized. God, could I have used that Simca that I was to pray for in that future Lincoln disaster on the Island. You don't hide a three-ton Lincoln Cosmopolitan in shiny black without a hood on Sea Island Drive very well but I tried to be as inconspicuous as possible. Well, as I approached the drive to Cottage 40, there was Susan in a Dior creation adorned with a Cartier pin. She was standing just outside the glassed-in porch. She didn't say "hey," she didn't say "welcome," she simply and very sternly said: **"In the Garage."**

This same Aunt once berated me for taking my cousins to Kentucky Fried Chicken on neighboring St. Simons Island. But, it's interesting how life can change one's values and sensibilities. By the time Susan became the executrix of Frank's estate and moved into 1177 in Moultrie, she and Uncle George had weathered some fairly drastic economic problems. She delighted in showing me a pre-pasted border from Wal-Mart chosen for one of the bathrooms! I never thought I would live to see the day. She also let me introduce her to the joys of a hot Crispy-

Crème donut in Montgomery, Alabama, when we motored over to see the Frank McCall Porcelain Collection at the Montgomery Museum of Fine Arts. Wait long enough; it all comes around.

In the summer, the Cloister Hotel would hire college students as waitpersons to replace their regular help who vacationed after the real season ended. I was lucky to be from Moultrie because Laura Dunn, *dahling*, was the Social Hostess at the hotel. She was tight with the personnel director, William Gibson, and I was a shoe-in.

I reported to the Cloister Hotel through a very different entrance that summer and lived in the employee barracks which made Fort Benning look like the Ritz-Carlton. Now, I shouldn't make such sweeping statements because just down the hall was Laura Dunn's compound. Once you got past the old white paneled door, you were walking on fine Sarouks and Herizes; there were beautiful English antiques everywhere, fine art, and a huge period mahogany carved bed that ensconced Miss Laura. She had a little refrigerator as well and would often call me up and invite me to have "a pomegranate, dahling" with her. She was a dead-ringer for Tallulah, and not just by speech alone.

After reporting to the dining room in my waiter's cutaway, I began training under a delightful waitress, Bobbie. Bobbie taught me willingly and gave me some good information (like slipping a fifth of *Wild Turkey* to Marvin—the egg man in the kitchen—so that I could get shirred eggs for my patrons).

After several days of training, I was allowed to go out on my own. We would always assemble in a spot between the two main dining rooms and our captains, Connie or Ethel would give us the run-down on what was featured on the evening's menu. Connie, who was an Irish red-headed no-nonsense pistol who used to keep Eugene O'Neil's Sea Island home in the summers, addressed our group and in a thick, clipped rendering of the blarney, announced, "Tonight is lobster night. If you have guests wishing lobster, please do the following: Secure a silver finger bowl for each guest and polish it thoroughly with your silversmith's mitt. Place a "Sea Island" paper liner in each bowl, fill it with tepid water to which you have added a slice of lemon, place a folded linen napkin over the bowl, then add a cracker." Wow—this was just great! I wasn't having to flame anything in cognac; this was going to be easy. I had a round table of eight delightful folks from Ohio and when I announced the lobster special, they all wanted in.

I got to work immediately—testing the water temperature with my fingers, going through hundreds of cut-up lemons in the boiler room kitchen to make sure there wasn't a "Sun-" or a "Kist" stamped on the rind, and after making eight of these assemblages, I opened the humidor and placed not one, but three saltines in a lovely stacked presentation, and promptly served the bowls—beaming all the time—to my table of Ohioans. Suddenly, from out of nowhere, I heard Connie's elevated brogue as she came towards me holding something that looked like what Dr. Whatley used to pull teeth with back home. She was holding it in her hand as if she was the assistant on *The Price Is Right*, but she wasn't smiling. "A *lobster* cracker, you fool; a ***lobster*** cracker!"

Well, I really wanted to take refuge at Fort Frederica. But my Ohio table was kind to me and good-humoredly asked the next morning for "lobster omelets, lobster marmalade, and lobster Danish." I managed to do just fine as a waiter and never had an accident, which is a wonder if you ever walked from the dining room—with the string orchestra playing potted palm hits—through the swinging doors onto something like a stage set for hell. There was food on the floor, people were screaming and tugging at the same plates, and steam seemed to come from everywhere. You were fired on the spot if you were caught eating anything—even a lobster cracker. We learned very quickly how to consume a melon ball cocktail or a crème brulee in one quick gulp. Our food in the employee's cafeteria only featured the dining room's left-over pastries. I lived that summer on key lime pie, napoleons, and an occasional pizza when we were able to get the hell off the Island, go to Brunswick and let our hair down over a bottle of Chianti, or better yet, go to the then down-at-the-heels King and Prince Hotel on nearby St. Simons Island and dance to *A Whiter Shade of Pale*.

The next summer, I got somewhat of a promotion, and I became the Junior Host at the Cloister working with two lovely girls, Carolyn Withers from Atlanta, and Linda Palenscar of Laverock, Pennsylvania. Laura Dunn was now my boss, and I just loved this woman. She could say "god-damn-it" while shod in her brown-and-white spectators with the most elegant but equally convincing delivery. She also knew that we began to beg for times to be away from all those South Georgia brats and a few impossible Yankee children thrown in for good measure. I still remember Yankee fathers fighting over little gold trophies from Taiwan for their sons in those horrible early morning pitch and putt tournaments. Laura would know that we had been "off the island" the night previous. So, she would set her Bailey, Banks and Biddle alarm clock, remove her satin blinders momentarily, and dial me up in the early a.m. to simply mutter—in her best Bankhead intonation: "Tooonament, dahling; tooonament."

Sometimes I didn't get sleep for other reasons. The Cloister's vice-president, Richard Everett, had a daughter who was the spitting image of Janis Joplin with a worse hair-do. She was the night telephone operator and she could ring your room continuously from the switchboard. Just one long riiiiiiiing on into the night. I couldn't complain about her since I reported to "Tricky-Dicky" myself, and if I answered, she filled the receiver with suggestive words of longing that I certainly wasn't in the mood, or the persuasion, for. I finally had to collect some extra pillows from some of my fellow waiters and stuff the phone under them when I came in at nights seeing a particular car at the telephone exchange building. The phone was hard-wired into the wall, wouldn't you know it?

I kept in close touch with my former waitpersons who had returned from last summer. Although I was now in a tuxedo many nights and dining at the tables at which I used to serve, I didn't have any reason to get my nose elevated. And to prove this, I decided to have a *little* party at Cottage 40. Carolyn and Alyce, Uncle Frank, and Dottie and Jerry Wright had all decided to go to the "Cloister Club" to a hippie costume affair. I asked for permission to have a few friends over, and got an ok. Well, when the dining room winded down, I invited all the kitchen staff, the wait staff, and any one else who was interested to "The Party at Cottage 40." Cars lined both sides of Sea Island Drive for several blocks and Uncle Frank's wicker liquor hamper got invaded. We had folks in every room of the house and we were having a fine time. Finally, our "hippie" authority figures returned from the Cloister and wasted no time in giving me hell and clearing out the "guests." What made it so memorable was to see the elegant Dottie Wright, dressed as some cross between a beatnik and Martha Raye shaking her finger at her daughter Janie, who had joined our merry-making. Somehow, in her costume, Dottie just wasn't really believable and we were overcome with the giggles. And Frank was not impressed with the liquor stock suddenly taking its leave either.

The next morning, Linda, Carolyn, and I received a very terse memorandum from Laura Dunn:

> TO: Junior Social Staff
> FROM: Laura Dunn
>   Please be reminded that the Junior Staff is not to date the help.

I remember Laura so fondly: our "Moon Landing Party" that we pulled off in the Cloister clubrooms, and the day she called me in distress to say that "the mould, dahling; the mould has invaded my apartment." You knew she was really tight with Bill Gibson, for when I got there, the electricians were already installing extra light bulbs in her closets. I had to hand-carry all her gowns and assorted threads to the cleaners while she patted and fanned herself in dismay. She dreaded evenings spent with rich Yankee women and would have much rather be regaling me with some stories of what "Son Bull" or "Son Holly" were doing—all the while embracing a nice Baccarat tumbler filled with good bourbon. She was an original and I miss her to this day.

I had a memorable summer, getting to know Tony Jacklin who had just won the British Open golf championship. I picked him up from the Brunswick Airport and promptly took him to McDonald's for breakfast. I didn't tell Aunt Susan about that one.

I once was able to have Frank on the Island to myself for a few hours as we motored down the one and only thoroughfare, Sea Island Drive. By this time Frank had become to Sea Island what Addison Mizner had been to Palm Beach and Boca Raton. He was a darling of the social set and his architecture pervaded the Island in countless aesthetic triumphs. One of those triumphs was a home for Mr. and Mrs. Milton St. John. This, what I call "Bermudian-Georgian" house was truly a remarkable residence, even if Frank and Mrs. St. John were at odds about things (I joined the club later when one of Frank's own employees, Johnny Shackelford, sided with her about some draperies I did exactly to her approved specifications). But back to our trip down the drive in Frank's Mercury Colony Park wagon. Frank was a bit bent over from the festivities of the previous night but he was hangin' in there. As we approached the beautiful St. John residence, from out of the hibiscus, oleander, and palmettos loomed all these spherical and trapezoidal forms across the street which belonged to the new creation of architect/developer John Portman. Portman is most famous for his cavernous lobby spaces with elevators traversing the entire height surrounded with "hanging gardens of Babylon" balconies. In his early days, after the creation of the Hyatt Regency Hotel in Atlanta, Carolyn, John and Frank were invited to the grand opening. Frank admonished, "For God sakes, whatevuh you do, don't look up; they'll know instantly that weah jest jawga crackuhs." To get Frank in a rolling boil, my father approached one of the round upholstered banquettes in the lobby and leaned down on the projecting back rest and exclaimed in his most "country-come-to-town" dialect, "I can't git any water out of these damn drinkin' fount'ins!" Portman's fantasies in architecture were particularly foreign to Frank's methodology, even inspiring such unsavory adaptations as those hideous ship foyers that Carnival Cruise Lines, for one, steers about in the ocean. In any event, we got to this spot of great contrast on Sea Island and I posed the question, "Frank, what do you think about John Portman's place?" Without missing a beat, he drawled, "I call it the *last* ride at Six Flags."

When Frank came to Winthrop University to do a lecture on his work, I couldn't resist taking him to near-by Fort Mill, South Carolina to P-T-L—the infamous empire built by Jim and Tammy-Faye Bakker. At the door of the Heritage Grand, Frank was kissed by a be-plumed doorman wearing a white vinyl belt and even whiter Corfam shoes. As Frank shuffled through the Portman-in-caricature lobby, complete with horrid reproduction Victorian furniture, constipated silk flower arrangements, Yankees in polyester leisure suits who had motored down in their Airstreams, and—worst of all—people being baptized in the hotel pool, he lifted his head up and uttered, "I've seen 'bout enuff."

Once while we were on the subject of architecture, excuse me— near-architecture—I asked Frank about his satellite operation on St. Simons Island. By this time, he had so many Sea Island commissions that it was practical to open a second office just to service those jobs. He sent one of his most talented (if not one of his snootiest), Johnny Shackelford, to head up the operation. I asked him, "Frank, how's your St. Simons office doing?" He replied, "You know, I'm really not shuah; all I can tell you is that Johnny's got a mighty fine taaan."

CHAPTER 6

The Big Paaaty, Part Two

WELL, NOW YOU know a bit about my mother and the dirt on a few other characters tripping the light fantastic on that specially-constructed dance floor at Brother's *Palazzo*. The fountain flowed, and the drinks flowed, and everybody flowed. It was a supper dance and a tasseled red-and-white striped canopy had been set up for serving the buffet. It's a wonder some of the guests didn't believe they had suddenly taken ill from the food for there appeared, in all her glory, Vera Zess (Moultrie's answer to Rose Marie on *The Dick Van Dyke Show*) with green hair. It was tinted a special avocado shade for the party to accent her white gown.

Yolande commented, "THE HOST spied Mrs. Bruce Schaefer of Toccoa. 'You've got on that red dress I like so much. Let's do the twist—but only after the orchestra plays my favorite piece, *September Song*. I can't explain why I like it, but I do.' " Now it is left to history how Mrs. Schaefer felt about that one, since all Atlanta now knew from reading *The Journal* that her dress was not purchased especially for the party. Dear Lord, it was something she already had! And if anyone could afford a new dress, it would be the Bruce Schaefer's of Toccoa. If Brother had visited them right after that affair, they might have helped him out onto the ledge of that town's famous waterfall!

My Aunt and Uncle, Mr. and Mrs. Ernest S. Tharpe, from Columbus, were there. My Aunt Sarah Tharpe was a more elegant version of Aunt Bee on the *The Andy Griffith Show*. A warmer, lovelier woman you could never know. I always loved her beautiful, ringing laugher around the mahogany table at "1177" (that's the Moultrie address of my grandparents and Uncle Frank. He kept the "1177 Southern Terrace" address long after the name was changed to "First Street" and I must admit I've done the same with the dilemma of "Crescent Drive" becoming a very pedestrian "Third Street"! Well, all that Crane's stationery from J. P. Stevens Engraving Company in Atlanta couldn't go to waste.)

And my Uncle George Patterson and his exquisite wife, my Aunt Susan, had come up from Savannah. My Aunt Susan had Uncle Frank's talent in spades; she was our Audrey Hepburn—and was equally elegant. Of course, Sherrod and Alyce were there to regale everybody with commentary about this villa that had suddenly overtaken part of their farm house plot.

Brother's brother, Jerry Wright and his wife Dottie were in tow. Dottie was the former Dorothy Mae Ogden of Atlanta and her childhood home was on prestigious West Paces Ferry Road. It became what is now Paces Academy. Dottie was always "my" movie star. After all, she reigned over a *Frank McCall* in Coral Gables with twelve bathrooms! She was every inch as beautiful as her look-a-like, Kim Novak. She was always especially warm and loving to me and I held her in great awe. Jerry Wright was one of the two Wright twins; Gene Wright was killed in World War II. Jerry was equally handsome as Brother, but more in a John Wayne-way. As a successful businessman who—in addition—married big money, he never lost his Moultrie sensibility. Sherrod and Alyce spared no time in cultivating the Jerry Wright's. Their trips to Coral Gables, and later to the Wright's home on Sea Island, or the large hunting ranch near Leesburg, Florida were legendary. And Alyce wasted not a minute in recounting those fabulous vacations—replete with the wanton and the wealthy. I drank it all up, feeling secure that Hollywood nor Palm Beach had anything on all this. When the last and current resident, Bill Remy Cole of Atlanta and Coral Gables took office at the *Palazzo*, Alyce was beside herself—and that will take another chapter. But skipping ahead a bit, early on, she was sizing this new bachelor up and asked Bill in a somewhat indignant tone, "Beeill, jes whea do you live in Cor'l Gables?" Bill responded in a very obliging and low-key voice, "Alyce, my house is on De Soto—one street over from Dorothy and Jerry's house on Granada. My house is directly across from *The Venetian Pool* (a magnificent water tableaux that resulted from mining coral rock for home construction—complete with gondola hitches, waterfalls, and towers enriched with pecky cypress beams; now on the National Register of Historic Places). Bill continued, "Alyce, when you and Sherrod went to see Dorothy and Jerry, did you ever go see the *Venetian Pool?*" Alyce came right back in a snarling delivery, "Beeill, when we went to Cor'l Gables, we went theah faw house paaatys; we didn't go theah to *sight-see!*" Well Bill Cole just loved this; a Warner Brothers screenwriter for Bette Davis couldn't have fashioned it any better.

There were numerous other Moultrie lovelies at Brother's soiree, and additional members of "The Moultrie Mafia"—a group of well-heeled and fun-loving couples who had retreated to Atlanta but always had their best times in Moultrie. Brother's aristocratic sister Harriett, and her husband, Dr. Mack Sutton of Albany, Georgia, were there too. And, Miss Bernice—long widowed—lent her Southern countenance over the proceedings.

Brother's supper dance ended in the wee hours; the children in "the bleachers" had long since gone to their beds and the paaaty of all paaatys came to an end. There were to be a few more grand affairs in the *Palazzo*, hosted by Brother, and then by its next owner, Colombian-born Juan Toro-Rico, but never on the scale of this one, and certainly none of them got the attention of the Atlanta papers.

CHAPTER 7

The End of Camelot

YOU WILL RECALL the quotation in *The Journal* by Brother about *September Song* and the fact that, unexplainably, he claimed it as one of his favorite pieces. Sadly, on *September* 24, 1984, Brother took his life.

I remember Brother talking to Glenn and me in Atlanta from his phone in the hospital room at Emory. Our house in Druid Hills was no further than three or four blocks from his bed. But it was the last time I heard his voice. He would not permit any visits in Atlanta and later barred everyone from the Cuban Mahogany doors of the *Palazzo* except his long time friend and sales manager at Wright Motor Company, Sam Perry.

When we talked, Brother was still upbeat and had that booming masculine voice, not unlike Rock Hudson's, somewhat intact. He said that he felt just awful and had no energy and that the team of doctors could not fathom what was wrong with him. Little did we know that he was possibly meeting the same fate as Rock but perhaps even more tragically. Brother was vain—and rightly so—and no one saw him in those final weeks when he was back in Moultrie. He used the front downstairs bedroom of the house as his sickroom and on the morning of September 24, he shot himself through a pillow. Del Richardson, his elegant and trusting cook and housekeeper, had to be the one to discover him. If there was any note or message, the family has never said anything about it.

I was, of course, devastated and so was Glenn—who thought Brother, next to Frank McCall, was the best thing since buttered bread. I left my job at Georgia State University in Atlanta to attend the funeral at Moultrie's Westview Cemetery where Brother joined his brother, Eugene, killed in action in 1944, his father, Robert Byrd Wright, who died in 1957, and his mother, Bernice, who left us in 1981.

Brother had been mighty good to his mother, Bernice, and in her final years, when health problems made her less ambulatory, Brother squired her everywhere in the 1977 Dove Gray Lincoln Continental Town Car which comfortably accommodated her wheelchair. I can remember, even after Bernice was wheelchair bound, that we would convene at the *Palazzo*, pour her a scotch and water, and put the LP of "Miss Peaches" on the stereo. Brother cared for his mother just as many other "men of color" have, and I am proud to be among those ranks myself.

The one spot of levity about an otherwise mournful day at the cemetery occurred when Carolyn and I approached the Wright family plot—graced by towering Italian Cedars which are still extant at this writing—and making our way under the funeral tent. Carolyn was dressed to kill of course, and Brother would have wanted that, but—low and behold—the Dove Gray Lincoln Continental pulled up and down came the power window in the rear compartment and Leo's wife, Maxie positioned her coiffured head just so, peered out of some designer sunglasses, and in the finest and most articulate English, said "Hello, Mrs. McCall." Carolyn was not upstaged exactly, but it was obvious that Maxie's tenure at 20 Tallokas Road had reinvented *her* wheel. Caring for Bernice and then for Brother at the *Palazzo* provided some uppity exposure that rubbed off.

It took a great deal of time for me to even begin to think about Brother's departure as I became aware that the *Palazzo* would never be the same again. The contents were divided by the family and a good deal of it was consigned to an antique shop on Saint Simons Island. The house was listed for sale and wisely, it was marketed in some of the more upscale national "boutique" realty publications.

The 1977 Lincoln Continental went to Brother's niece, Dottie's daughter Janie. (Many years later I arranged for it to be sold to my close friend, Robert Carpenter of Rutherfordton, NC where it resides to this day and is affectionately named "Miss Bernice". I don't know where in the hell Brother's beautiful Continental Mark II went. But, curiously, this would not be the only Mark II to grace the *Palazzo*. More on that later.)

Brother left behind not only the *Palazzo* as his legacy, but his mark was found in significant contributions to Georgia's Public Broadcasting System, Georgia's educational system, the Colquitt County Regional Hospital, the formation of American Banking Company (now Ameris Bank), and a score of other endeavors.

The *Palazzo* did not sit vacant for too long due to the national exposure afforded the property by good advertising and the particularly modest price for a home that could not have been duplicated for hundreds of thousands of dollars more than the asking figure. The house caught the attention of Juan G. Toro-Rico of Colombia, South America and Miami and soon, Juan became the new owner and Alyce's most unusual neighbor. But there was some consistency; Juan indeed was "colorful" too, or to use the term from *Steel Magnolias*, he had "track lighting"…and several pods at that.

At home with Juan, Carolyn, and me, Hahira, GA, 1992.
Robert Carpenter

CHAPTER 8

The Toro-Rico Regime

JUAN'S, AND HIS partner, Jim's possessions had hardly been unpacked at the *Palazzo* before Alyce was establishing her neighborhood autonomy and Sherrod was making sure that all of Juan's insurance needs were being serviced at Harper-McCall. Juan was a diminutive creature with a shock of black hair and a somewhat unkempt mustache. His partner, Jim, was a Southern boy and strikingly handsome. Jim's time at the *Palazzo* was short-lived as he became the second person to die (definitely of "the plague") in the mansion on October 3, 1989. Sherrod and Alyce were on call night and day (Juan was a night person personified) to assist Juan as Jim began to falter. Since Juan was Colombian and even though he lived in Miami previously—that certainly doesn't qualify one to have lived in the United States, *or, at least Georgia*. So, Alyce and Sherrod became Juan's attaches and helped him with his every move.

Mr. Juan G. Toro-Rico, born in 1952, came from a wealthy family who had made their money in a chain of department stores in Colombia. I had the opportunity to meet his parents and they were lovely, exceedingly refined people. Juan had been given all the best educational opportunities in his native land and in the states. His talents were formidable in the arena of the theatre, costume design, and dance. Now, Juan's talents did not extend to interior decoration and the horrors that he drug into the once beautifully furnished *Palazzo* looked like they had been selected from the gift section of the Swiss

Colony catalogue. But dance? My, could Juan dance! And it didn't take long for Carolyn McCall to find this out. Alyce may have wielded a great deal of power over Juan, even to the extent of being the recipient of some *very* Spanish jewelry that made Kim Novak's necklace worn by Madeline in *Vertigo* look like it came from a Sarah Coventry party. Yes, Alyce may have had Juan in her pocket, but not on the dance floor. I believe that there was a bit of jealousy on her part at any function that featured dancing because Carolyn and Juan really were an item. By this time, my father had put down the bottle for good, consuming himself with game hunting and his job with the Hitchcock Corporation—both of which somehow seemed to be the same occupation. He was rarely at any Moultrie social functions, but when he was commandeered by Carolyn, he would actually tend bar and also mimic his former foolish drunken self, and sometimes the silly antics of other Moultrians who experienced an unfortunate metamorphosis when they imbibed. So, this left Carolyn free to be Juan's Ginger Rogers, and everybody, except Alyce, was happy—including my Daddy.

The most memorable dancing exhibition ever mounted by the team of Toro-Rico and McCall was at Moultrie's Arts Center (a brainchild of Uncle Frank's). It was the evening of the Patron's Ball and there was a live orchestra. Juan was smartly outfitted in his tuxedo and Carolyn had on something memorable. They were doing a Latin step, after having several cocktails, and somebody in the team got wobbly and they landed on the ballroom floor in perfect missionary position. Carolyn, of course, got the giggles and infected Juan and a flock of patrons (including me) circled around for what seemed ten minutes, raising the ballroom ceiling with laugher, while the infamous dance team held their suggestive posture on the hardwood floor. Glenn Thomas once said of my mother that you could put her in a room and in five minutes she would have lassoed every gay man present. She did seem to have a magnetic "gay-dar" that was unfailingly accurate. At one of Frank's *Fabulous Welcome to Spring* benefits, she once remarked to Glenn, "Isn't that an attractive man over there? I wonder *who* does his hair?"

I became somewhat of a regular guest at Juan's (Carolyn and I had moved to Hahira, Georgia near Valdosta by this time) and I was invited to several of his lavish parties at the *Palazzo*. Juan wisely had contracted with Jim Jordan of my uncle's architectural office to complete the unfinished ballroom on the second floor. Jim Jordan was one of many talented apprentices who went on to make a name for themselves in architecture and architectural design. Jim was, perhaps, one of the most talented—and certainly one of the most adoring of Frank. His Frank McCall imitations were legendary. Before Jim met an untimely death in 2008 at the prime of his professional life, he had accumulated many "Uncle Frank stories". One of the best was about the day he came to interview for a job with Frank. Jim had just graduated from the School of Architecture at Georgia Tech and his singular dream was to work for the office of William Frank McCall, Jr. Back then, Frank's office was in the first McCall family home (prior to 1177) on Hillcrest. This nineteen-twenties bungalow-style house was a disorganized but somehow elegant place with a simple metal sign propped up by the front entrance. It was exceedingly crowded, but crowded with very talented men including Jack Wilson, Vernon Ogletree, Charles Ryan, and later, John Hand, Neil Turner, and Allen Shumake. I had the great fortune during my high school days to work there as a file clerk and one of the "men-Fridays" (everyone on Frank's staff was a "man-Friday"). I can still smell the redolent vapors of Maxwell House coffee and rubber erasers, and yes, the ammonia in the blueprint machines. I can also hear the sounds of Barbra Streisand, Judy Garland, Ella Fitzgerald, Nat King Cole, and—of course—'ole Blue Eyes. Back then, this music played on a small stereo phonograph daily.

So, in this setting, Jim Jordan appeared in coat and tie for his interview with Frank. He was probably ushered in by Frank's loyal secretary (I use the term *loyal* in jest), Pat Wilson, to Frank's "office"— actually an elegant living room consumed by a large rent table at its epicenter and festooned with a large glass Moorish star pendant above. Frank had his head down and was in deep study and muttered, "Come on in." Jim and Frank talked a little—mostly chit-chat—and Frank, never changing his position—said, "Well, I guess you'd bettah come on in to wuuk Munday." Jim was thrilled but remained puzzled about Frank's devotion to something seemingly more important than the interview. As he made his exit, he purposely walked 'round the table behind Frank. Our architect was intently studying a new Brooks Brothers catalogue that had come in the mail. I don't think they ever had eye contact until that following Monday.

Jim did a fine job for Juan on the ballroom of the *Palazzo*. Juan's engraved party invitations always specified that no furs or ivory were to be worn at his galas in the new room. His buffets were served by waiters in white gloves and it was Moultrie's true *haute couture* event each year. But, despite all the elegance, despite a finished ballroom, it was never like that of Brother's world. Alyce didn't seem to care in the least because she had Juan's every move under her thumb. She was so controlling that once, when Jim Jordan, Juan, and I decided to go to Atlanta on a self-guided Philip Shutze architectural tour, Alyce informed me that I should not leave my car parked in the front courtyard of the *Palazzo*. People might talk.

After Juan's Jim died, Juan had a brief change of mode. He got married!—to a *woman*! This union was so transparent to me that I just couldn't believe Juan was planning to go through with it. He had seemed to be quite content with just his dog, *Bernard*—a Saint Bernard, of course, and the antics of Alyce and assorted friends. When he would walk *Bernard*, it really was the other way around. I still have memories of Juan being tugged on a leash as he rounded the big shaped boxwoods around the *Palazzo* (Bill Cole called the shrubbery *peters and balls*, for between each pair of rounded boxwood, there would be a taller, more cylindrical one).

My Tiffany vase had hardly reached the mansion before I found out that the union between this Latin beauty and Juan had been annulled. My take is that, on the wedding night, Juan and Bernard went up the stairs to one bedroom, and *Madame X* was sent to quite another. Whatever the case, the female occupation at the *Palazzo* was a very brief one and cleared the way for perhaps the most unbelievable story that has ever unfolded within the pilastered limestone facade of "the house on Alice B. Toklas."

By this time, Alyce had become almost inseparable from one of the dearest, purest magnolia blossoms in all of Georgia, Ida Murphy.

Ida is also about the most beautiful "substantial" woman that I have ever encountered and one of the wittiest. She emulated the role of the "straight" part of the Alyce-and-Ida vaudeville team, and when they paired up, and got a bit "organized" (as my *scotcheroo* mother put it), they were indescribably funny. Their friendship, of course, went much further than displays of Southern levity; they were really there for each other, in the good times and the not-so-good. Ida also began to enjoy a tight friendship with Juan. Alyce may have provided an initial introduction, but Ida captivated Juan (as she does most anyone) using her own particular charm and wit. With her husband Wandell deceased and her lovely daughters doing their own thing, she had the time to travel, socialize, and *paaaty* with Juan, Alyce and Sherrod. They became permanent fixtures on the Toro-Rico list of approved personages and at times even doled out advice—much of it good—to Juan, although he rarely listened. Surely, they must have advised against this ill-conceived union that lasted less than a week, but, alas, Juan went through with it, then promptly absolved it.

With the house clear of any unnecessary players, Juan returned to a quiet normalcy and made his daily outings with Bernard (who was NOT on Alyce's good list; they got off to a bad start from the get-go after he relieved himself in her yard).

Right after Juan's betrothed was banished from the *Palazzo*, Bernard developed a serious hip problem. I am convinced that this was no accident; I really believe "that woman" pushed him down the staircase in a fit of jealousy. In any event, the dear dog died. Juan was, of course, consumed with grief and immediately began to make plans for a wake, a service, and burial of his dear (and perhaps only completely faithful) friend.

Earlier that year, Juan had been accused of "money laundering" and the *Palazzo* received another brand of newspaper exposure much different from that linked to Brother Wright. Juan was eventually cleared of all wrong-doing, but you can just imagine the bumper-to-bumper traffic that erupted as the populace rubber-necked a glimpse through the entrance gates of what they believed to be a private branch of Fort Knox. In other words, it was not particularly good timing for the tragedy, or comedy that unfolded around Bernard's death.

After Bernard expired, Juan called Harrell Funeral Home in what he thought would be an everyday, usual request to have Bernard embalmed and fitted to a fine casket (we're talking human proportions here). Juan was incensed when he received a response at the other end of the line, "I'm sorry, sir, but we don't *work* on dogs." It was in the heat of the summer when all this marital and canine upheaval was intensifying so Juan was left in a particularly disturbed mood. By the time he called me in Hahira to deliver the news and beg that I come and help him receive bereaved visitors, he had managed to wrestle a lovely mahogany casket out of Carl Harrell, but Bernard's needs on the embalming table were out of the question.

By the time I reached the *Palazzo* there were mourners coming and going. I am not kidding. Many were even dressed in black and were greeted by more black at the front door which was festooned with a funeral wreath. I couldn't believe it as I mounted the steps and greeted Harriett and James Whelchel who had done their vigil and were leaving. Juan was in "morning mourning" clothes and was somber to a fault. As I entered the foyer I could smell the burning of more candles than the local Catholic Church could have ever rounded up. And there, in living color, as I entered the *grande salon* to my left, lay poor Bernard, clutching a red rose in his paws, sleeping serenely in a polished casket near the fine Italian mantle Frank had carefully designed. Oh yes, there was a guest register and everything. I immediately volunteered to tend bar mainly because I needed a drink my ownself in order to ponder the unreality of the moment.

Juan implored me to call Julian Bridges, a local florist, to see why the spray for the casket had not arrived. Julian filled the phone with goings on: the so-and-so's wedding, and so-and-so's funeral *ad nauseam*, but yes, he and his partner Bill (Alyce always called him Julian's "side-kick") would be over shortly with the spray. Spray? It was more like a *torrent* of roses and *leather-leaf fern* (don't ever give any flowers to Carolyn with that in the arrangement, especially not in heaven!).

Just as the spray was appropriately placed on the casket illuminated by candlelight and little else, Alyce and Sherrod appeared. Alyce didn't have her feet past the first marble tile inside the foyer before she said under her breath, waving her hands towards the *salon*, "I'm not gonna cry ovah that damned dawg; Johnny get me a C.C. and Seven." And she was true to her word. She used the drink-fetching to get into the English Study with Sherrod and she never went anywhere else. Of course, Juan relocated from his *chambre des morts* to be with Alyce and Sherrod. Alyce immediately and demonstratively said, "Juan, you've got to get this dawg in the ground immeegetly. We're in the middul of the summah!." Juan replied in his thick Anglo-Colombian accent, "I know, Aleeece, I haff to poot my poor Bernarh in ze groun soon."

I had Anne Smith in tow. Now as a good friend of Juan's she had reason to put a check on her grief as Bernard had once relieved her of a good chunk of her posterior after a disastrous dinner party at the *Palazzo* when the dog decided that Anne was a runaway best appetizer on the menu. It was really a serious bite—confirmed by Dr. Thomas Estes—and no one can explain why in the hell Bernard had such a mood swing. He was always a prince with me and most everyone else. But Anne managed a tear or two (it may have been tears of final relief) and tried her best to console Juan as she watched the countless comings and goings of those in black. She was probably most intent on trying to fathom how this canine had been wrestled into a casket by his master who Anne described as "soaking wet he might weigh a hundred pounds and stand five feet, two inches tall." She, at least, could say goodbye to any more Tetanus shots!

Alyce got her way—all the way. Since the funeral home would not allow Bernard to be interred in their memorial garden, Juan decided to bury his dearly departed in the front courtyard of the *Palazzo*—on Alyce's side. He managed to get a regular funeral tent with "Harrell Funeral Home" emblazoned on the skirting. Now, how does one literally stop traffic on Alice B. Toklas? Try stationing Alyce and Ida, in their best black suits and hats, under a funeral tent with Juan, dressed in an even more dramatic mourning ensemble, whilst a human-sized casket is lowered into the ground. According to Anne Smith, Carl Harrell's equipment operators conducted the service; the Catholic priest declined to preside. Try doing that on the heels of a money-laundering charge that already had 'em coming by—night and day. Allegood's must have sold a lot of bar-b-que that week.

Anne, having a very special "bond" with Bernard recounts the rest of the saga better than I, and with her permission, I quote:

"Carl Harrell leads me to part two of this tale. A local female veterinarian (Dance Mom) calls another Mom (slightly flustered and often "out-to-lunch"). [*The following conversation ensues:*]

> *Vet: Have you heard that Bernard died and Juan is arranging for a casket and a funeral?*
>
> *Mom: So sorry to hear that Bernard (**the dance teacher at the Arts Center**) died and nice that Juan is paying for everything. (Why would Juan need to pay for the funeral of the dance teacher?)*
>
> *Vet: Need to ask a favor. Carl Harrell refuses to embalm Bernard and we need lots of dry ice to cool the body until the funeral. [The mom at the other end of the phone is married to a wholesale grocer.] Can Tommy help us…?*
>
> *Mom: He doesn't deal with frozen foods and I don't think I can come up with that amount of dry ice, or regular ice, for that matter. (What was wrong with Bernard that Carl won't embalm him? Where do they have him laid out? How horrible!)*
>
> *Vet: Well, since you can't help with the ice could you put him in your big freezer at the house?*
>
> *Mom: I don't think so. The freezer is full. (I don't want a dead body in my freezer—especially one Carl won't embalm. Plus, what if the kids opened the freezer and found their dance teacher?)*
>
> *Vet: Thanks. Guess we will just have to do the best we can.*

[The temporary solution to the physics of keeping the dog preserved and the mourners happy was for Juan to turn his thermostat down to its lowest point. Anne was among many whose hands began to turn blue during the wake.]

Anne continues:

"Dance Mom continued to watch the newspaper each day for information about Bernard's death and the announcement of services. She became more upset that Bernard was not getting the proper respect and attention. At the end of the week she attended a dinner party. During the pre-dinner conversation she overheard bits of another conversation nearby: 'Bernard, casket and flowers and DOG. DOG she gasped as the fog lifted on the events of the last week while the dinner guests shook with laughter.' Months later—even though Carl was unable to provide complete funeral services, his men delivered and positioned a fine marble headstone on Alyce's side."

CHAPTER **9**

Landin' In the Tallahassee Mud

AFTER BERNARD'S DEATH, Juan was not the same. He did take on a new partner, Dennis, but I don't think Dennis was enamored of Moultrie and the idea of large-scale pseudo-heterosexual parties was just not on his agenda. Juan continued to see Alyce and Ida and a few other close friends. By 1991, Frank was in bad shape. The man who had a thousand friends and had mastered the art of attracting clients who were also on his social list and he on theirs, was really destitute when it came to having a bosom buddy.

I tried to be Frank's confidante but the openness and acceptance of my own orientation was unsettling to a man who had come up in a generation that kept that part locked away. He was very pleased that I had moved from college administration into the field of interior design, first as a campus planner and later professor of interior design at Winthrop University in South Carolina. Now, as a private practitioner, I could see Frank often as Hahira was just a forty minute drive from Moultrie. He loved coming to visit Carolyn and me and he was always complimentary of our little "Doris Day" cookie cutter house, where I treated him to movies like the Garland-Mason epic, *A Star Is Born*.

While Juan was still around, Miss Ida invited Carolyn, Frank, Sherrod and Alyce, Juan, and me for one of her exquisite dinner parties. She would always bring in Del Richardson (who was Brother's former cook and housekeeper) to preside in the kitchen, and the collaboration of those two gourmands was truly memorable. In the week past, Deen

Day Smith (who was the widow of Cecil Day, the Day's Inn visionary) had escaped a very near brush with death when several family members and other friends, including Moultrie artist Lynwood Hall, crashed in the Berrien Straits. (Deen had married Charles Owen Smith, Jr. after she lost her first husband and funneled a huge amount of money into making his plantation home, *Iris Court*, one of the finest antebellum landmarks in the South.) There were some fatalities in Deen's entourage and the *Moultrie Observer* had devoted an entire section to the story.

I felt somewhat ill-at-ease that night and Juan didn't seem to want to involve me in any discourse, and Frank—poor Frank; he was slumped over in a chair with his mouth half open and he'd manage a grunt or two and that was about it. He was on a "no-alcohol" regimen so I fixed him a "play drink" of club soda, bitters, and lemon. (Little did I know that his "no-alcohol" pronouncement was from the doctor, and not from Frank; he was hitting the scotch at 1177 heavily, according to Jim Jordan). At the other end of the room—you guessed it—Alyce and Sherrod had wrestled control of the paaaty conversation. I was not interested in whatever they were picking apart, accessorizing their commentary with much body language and hand waving. So I just sat there. Frank just sat there. And Juan might have just as well evaporated into thin air.

Ida passed by on the way to the powder room and I asked if she had a copy of the special section of *The Observer* and she replied, "Yeah, sugah; I'll get it for you right now-ow." (Ida can usually get at least two syllables out of a one syllable word). She brought me the paper and I was immediately overcome with the seriousness of the air disaster. I had no idea that it had been that bad (although I first read about it in *USA Today*). I got a bit glassy-eyed and quietly put the newspaper under my chair. At that exact moment, Big A caught my eye from the other end of the room. This veteran *paaaty grande dame* could be in the middle of a discourse and still sense what was shakin' with every other person in a room.

She knew I was upset, and she said, "Darlin', what you readin'?" I replied, "Alyce, it's the special edition of the paper about "The Crash" and it is definitely not party material." And, at that moment, she went into paaaty overdrive, determined to bring me right out of my despair. "That's nothin' sugah, 'till you heah 'bout MY plane crash!"

Judy Garland often felt a "...Song Comin' On", but tonight, Alyce was onstage and we knew she had a "Story Comin' On". It was kind of like the waters parted in the middle of Ida's living room and everybody rearranged themselves in their chairs and got ready for her delivery. I knew how to kick-start her by asking, "What plane crash, Alyce?" "Why sugah," she said as her eyes looked heavenward, "when we landed in the Tallahassee muudd." (Alyce was just behind Ida in the art of *syllability*).

I had already begun to crack up (Frank was still seemingly out of it), so I continued, "Please, Alyce...do tell." "Well we were goin' jest right along (at this juncture, she outstretched her arms and dipped and swooped as if there were some problems with the ailerons) and I had a young guul sittin' with me who'd never flown befoah. I said, honey, jest buckle uupp, auwdah you a nice cocktail, and I'll show you how it's done. I've flown lots a times (I couldn't help but think of Prissy's empty promises to Scarlett in *Gone With the Wind*)."

Alyce continued—now that she had everyone in the palm of her hand excepting her brother-in-law, "We were jest goin' right along when suddenly the capt'in came on the "loudspeaker" and said that we were experincin' a lil' problum. And, sugah, 'bout that time all the skillets from the kitchen came rollin' down the aisle!" Alyce used her arms to demonstrate the pillage of all that Southern cookware; I envisioned cast iron fry pans with corn pone and collard greens going splat! all over the fuselage. "And honey I want you to know, we missed the runway and landed in the Tallahassee muudd!"

We were hysterical by then and Alyce continued: "There were all kinds of flashin' lights and men in raincoats and we had to slide down a big yellah "innah tube" to the groun'! Well, we slid right on out and I got all this foam all over muh best suit and got to the middul of the *runway* and called yah Uncle Sheuud up." Now, Sherrod had been sitting there, giving Alyce the entire floor—which was a singular event in itself, but at that point he spoke up and said, "Alyce, I think you mean the *concourse*." She retorted, "Well, whatevah it was, I was in the middul of it! And I rung yah Uncle Sheuud up". She put her left hand to her ear and used her right arm to crank the phone. I thought my, my Tallahassee must be backward!

Once Alyce got through crankin' and ringin' she said, "Sheuud, this is Alyce. I've been in a *horribul* plane crash!" Even at this point, while others were pounding Ida's Hamadan, Frank was still in la-la land. Alyce continued, "Yes, a *horribuuul* crash." "Well where are you callin' from Alyce...*heaven?*" queried Sherrod. At that very moment, Frank focused on the room and grunted with his Southernmost tinge of sarcasm, "Well, that sho was a compliment!"

CHAPTER 10

The Arrival of Monsieur Cole

IT WAS NOT long after Ida's dinner party that Juan informed Alyce he was putting the *Palazzo* up for sale and was moving back to Miami. I'm sure Alyce and Ida were at a loss over this and Sherrod was facing a nice package of insurance policies that were to be no more.

Juan left quietly, with little fanfare, prior to selling the mansion. With him he took about every light fixture the electricians could loose. I particularly remember the dining salon with its magnificent plaster medallion sporting a bare light bulb!

In January of 1995, the *Palazzo* welcomed its third owner, Bill Remy Cole. If the former owners of the place were interesting characters, then Bill—or *Monsieur Cole*, as we are apt to call him—is a presentation in Cinemascope and color by DeLuxe. Actually aside from the times when the *Monsieur*, a.k.a. Bill Remy Cole does recitatives on dialogue from *Hush, Hush Sweet Charlotte* and *Sordid Lives*, he's a fairly everyday run-of-the-mill kind of guy—well, at least in *our* world. My friend, Michael Kelly bestowed the *Monsieur Cole* title on him because when we visited him in Coral Gables (after a disastrous inaugural I made on my own earlier), Bill was on an art and antiques buying kick that would have convinced you he was out of the top drawer of the French aristocracy. Seriously, we made a cook's tour of almost every antique house in the city and he made a purchase or two. One of them was a rather nice painting. Michael asked if he might examine it and the *Monsieur* looked at him, pulled his arms into his chest cavity, put on his best protective guise and said, "Oh no, honey, this is *muh* paintin'!"

Alyce told me that a gentleman from Atlanta had purchased the *Palazzo* and that's about all I knew until the death knell issued by Alyce—full of despondency and infuriation—which she delivered via telephone: "Johnny, git ovah heah quick. This ma-an is unloadin' ole' Cadillacs in the courtyard and I jest won't have it; I'm not havin' a used caah lot on Tallokas!" Well, this was enough to get my curiosity up and old cars have always been a passion of mine, so I departed Hahira bound for Moultrie post haste. When I got to Alyce's she was on her front walk and she looked me straight in the eye with a fire and furor that even Joan Crawford could not have mustered and said, "I'll tell you one thing…I'm not breakin' in anothuh wun!" I guess Alyce already had Bill's number.

As I gazed through the fence I didn't see Cadillacs but rather some lovely Imperials and a Continental Mark II (curiously, this was the second rare Mark II to board at the *Palazzo*). "Alyce, I said in an attempt to be consoling, "those aren't Cadillacs—they're Imperials." "Well, I don't give a damn what they are, I'm not havin' 'em!" Evidently, she hadn't even considered the insurance possibilities for Sherrod at that point.

It was a rocky start and it got rockier. Early on, Bill's big dog, named *Brother* of all things, decided to leave a calling card in Alyce's grass. And Bill offered not even one cubic zirconia to soften the blow! He was not intimidated in the least by Alyce, and certainly he had more money. Bill was the only child of a family that had made their fortune in blast furnaces in Chicago and also the Cole Stove Works in Atlanta. It was good, old money and Bill never really had to hit a lick at a snake, concentrating instead on fine antiques and art, jewelry, classic cars, and building an important doll collection.

Alyce could already tell that an evening of cocktails and country ham and biscuit was not going to give her any leeway with Mr. Cole. For me, our relationship centered around the cars and the genuine love he had for the history of the house. As a child, he often went to movies at the Atlanta Paramount and the façade and all its trappings meant something to him. His grandparents were early settlers of the Miami area; in fact, their home and surrounding property became the Coral Reef Yacht Club in Coconut Grove. He loved fine architecture and already owned one of the most architecturally important homes in Coral Gables. These things put us on a good footing, not to mention that we both had a passion for classic cars and the history of his Paramount-borne *Palazzo*.

When I became defensive of Bill, Alyce just fumed and immediately changed the subject. Somewhere along the way, the Ginkgo tree in Bill's yard shed its leaves as nature intended and the majority of them fell in Alyce's side garden. Alyce evidently had Juan trained to catch them in his hands or something every fall. Bill's gardener waited too long to suit Alyce, so her list of grievances was mounting.

Then, the floodgates burst. I never seemed to be in Moultrie when there was another holocaust, so again, I got the same kind of supercharged phone call: "Johnny get ovah heah right now; Beeill is paintin' the fence a bright orange!" Earlier, Alyce had actually asked me to pay a courtesy visit to Bill after he mentioned that he wanted to "touch up" the fence—the right side of which was at her level of vision and property line. I did so, and suggested that Bill repaint the fence in a dark "Charleston Green"—which is a rich tint appropriate for even a Palladian mansion. So, when I got her hysterical call, I reassured her: "Alyce, I've already consulted with Bill just as you asked me, and the color I suggested is a dark black-green; I'm sure that's just the metal primer that the painters are applying prior to the first coat." "No," she retorted, "that's the finul culah and it's orange—jest like the highway men waeauh!"

Well, she was right. Bill got it in his head that because this lovely shade of "Bittersweet" had worked so well in his Mediterranean home in Coral Gables, it would just be perfect for the *Palazzo*. I tried in vain to explain to Bill that this was a whole different architectural ballgame, but he became mesmerized by all the attention and antics of Alyce, the neighborhood, and anyone else who would listen to her vocal fireworks. *Alyce's Bittersweet Lament*, for a time, superseded *Juan's Fable of St. Bernard* and took over spot number one on the Cocktail Talk Circuit in Moultrie. The fence remained orange for a time until Bill came to his senses and chose a nice, somber dark gray to replace it. Thank God, for he had even gone so far as to add touches of this jack o'lantern orange on the overdoor of the front entrance!

Alyce became Bill Cole's Betty Davis on a rampage. And the uglier she was to Bill, the more infatuated he was with Alyce. He'd love to hear her slip out with tales of paaaty's and other social affairs which never included him and he'd put on his best melancholy act and respond by saying, "I guess I'm just not suitable." He could have cared less about going to them anyway and the surgical support hose he wore to walk the dog would not be appreciated by Moultrie's Savile Row.

The *Monsieur* and me at his Coral Gables home.
Michael Kelly

Speaking of paaaty's, Alyce had one to which I insisted my brother take my mother. I just about had all the transporting I could handle that week. After Carolyn suffered a massive stroke, she did not slow down with her social functions. I had moved her to Moultrie to the old Colquitt Hotel which had become a retirement care facility. To make sure things were good for Carolyn, I sold our home in Hahira, and occupied several suites on the third floor of the building. I took her everywhere in that wheelchair and we continued to have a lot of fun.

But on this particular night, I had begged off. Alyce had a slew of people and there was very little parking to be had on the curb at her house or driveway, so the cars naturally found their way to the front of Bill's house as well. In the midst of Alyce's paaaty, her uniformed maid came to the living room and said, "Mrs. McCall, you're wanted on the phone." Alyce, probably in the middle of a tall tale, snorted back, "Well who IS IT?!" "Well, ma'am it's Bill Cole." "God-damn it; 'scooze me, I'll be right back," she bellowed to her circle of guests.

She grabbed the phone like she was trying to strangle it, uttering a very ugly "Hello!" Bill said, "Alyce, this is Bill (as if she didn't already know)." Alyce, cutting him off at the quick, yelled, "Beeill, can't you see I'm in the middul of a paaaty?" Bill, rather glibly replied, "Well, I just thought you might want to know that one of your guests left the lights on in their Cadillac." Alyce, who suddenly sounded like she was teaching vacation bible school said, "Oh, thank you so very much!" She then hung up the phone and returned to the C.C. and Seven she had workin'.

CHAPTER 11

R.I.P.

I CAN'T TELL you the countless times Alyce would have me over and say, "Johnny, put sumthin' good on the HI-FI and fix me a C.C. and Seven". The HI-FI indeed! When I'd greet her, she would consistently point to a particular spot on her face for me to plant my kiss. Actually, Alyce was not particularly touchy-feely but her *joie de vivre* made up for any shortcomings in that department. And she was the very essence of Christmas.

Saying goodbye to most of the characters on which this book is founded was difficult for me. After losing my grandparents on both sides, my father was the first major player to go, on August 3, 1982. I was living in South Carolina then and when I made my way to Moultrie directly to our "new" house on First Street, I couldn't even find a parking place. I walked into a typical Moultrie jam of a stand-up cocktail party. It just didn't hit me right at first and I turned around and started to make my way out in the yard when Joyce Kirk buttonholed me and said, "Now, Johnny you need to understand that your mother has cared for your father from his bedroom in the house for ages now and it's time to celebrate your father's life and Carolyn's release." She was dead-on-the-money after I thought about it. My father's battle with colon cancer had not been easy for either of my parents, and yes, it was time to move on. The regrettable part about my father's passing was that after he put down the bottle, he and Carolyn fell hopelessly back in love with each other, but it was only for a short while in the continuum of things. They pursued their own passions and communicated primarily by notes under magnets on the refrigerator. But my mother saved every scrap my father ever placed there. He really made them works of literary and pictorial art. My favorite was a valentine to Carolyn showing her dressed in some sort of S&M outfit with leather leggings and Nancy Sinatra boots. And yes, there was some embittered reference to "C-Island".

I would miss Daddy's routine of smoking one Camel followed by a Newport chaser, while dressed only in his underwear. He did this almost every night of his life. I never saw him with a cigarette at any other time. I missed his early—and astute—observation that commercial television was nothing but a manipulative and highly shallow venture with little artistic merit. He would always wait in the wings until Carolyn was totally wrapped up in something like *Playhouse Ninety*, and—just when the two actors were ready to go upstairs and view the etchings—he would come to Carolyn, get right in her face, and say *"rugus pugus"*. This was Daddy's self-constructed Southern-Latin term describing that something sexual was about to go on. I never heard anything that did a better job of indicating that particular kind of situation unless it was Berrien Cheatham's remark when asked about how two people had fared on their numerous dates: "Well," he said with his little pinky lifted above a glass of scotch, "I think they've had *carnival knowledge* of each other."

Uncle Frank left us on March 12, 1991 and he died a very lonely man. He literally drank himself to death. Many of his closest friends and colleagues refused to believe it, but I knew the truth. I often blamed myself for not just taking him by the reigns and saying "this is how it's gonna be from now on". But I realize now that was a shallow proposition; he had already chosen a death wish, fueled by untold loneliness. He had tried a second, long-distance relationship with Hank Stembridge, a professor of interior design at The Savannah College of Art and Design, but that didn't really blossom into a full-fledged union. Low and behold, Hank turned out to be the childhood neighbor and friend of my pal Robert Carpenter who grew up with Hank in Forest City, North Carolina. Hank's father was a minister at the First Baptist Church the Carpenter's attended. When we discovered this, Uncle Frank did not seem to be particularly amused, and the evening we convened at *The Hedges* left him somewhat out to pasture while Hank, his lovely mother, and Robert recalled old times.

Prior to Hank, my uncle had a "first" relationship that I can document. (This was in addition to a long standing courtship of convenience with a fine Southern lady, Peggy Popper of Macon). Charles Buffington, formerly of Atlanta, "lived" in Moultrie in an antique shop that Frank had established in Julian Bridges' old floral shop. The McCall family seemed to accept this in stride and Charles was constantly with Frank until the tide turned—literally. On one of the encampments at Cottage 40, Frank, in a very inebriated state began to lay verbal assaults on Charles during a midnight swim in the nearby ocean. Although I was not a part of this ploy by Charles to probably sober Frank up, I had witnessed my uncle when he drank to excess. Every ugly thought he had seemed to make its way to the top, just as it had in all the years my father hit the bottle. It was a very unsavory McCall trait.

Uncle Frank and Peggy Popper.
Collection of the Author

My father, for example, would often come in from a bout at the Country Club and slump into the wingback by the front door and say in the most diabolical voice imaginable, "Get gone!" This would be after he had left the car door open in his Pontiac and the bag of beer brought from the club would have sweated so that the cans began rolling down our driveway onto Camellia Drive. One night, when I was being brought home by some friends after an MYF function, the headlights of their car caught the eyes of my Daddy, sitting upright in the flowerbed facing us. Or how about the time Carolyn hid John's car keys and he got so desperate that he hailed my English bicycle and tried to make a run to the Sunset Country Club? He didn't know about the brake levers mounted on the handlebar so he went off into a deep chasm at the foot of our street. Remember, it is easy to tell these stories about *my* father because later he became a new man and my love and respect for him grew so that I forgave him for not being a father to me when I really needed him. He did try but there were too many demons competing. With Willie's age difference, there was a very different arrangement and my brother was able to enjoy many good years with Daddy long after the drinking days. They loved hunting together and William eventually took my father's job when Daddy became bedridden.

But, back to Frank. After that fateful evening swim at Sea Island, Frank returned to Moultrie black and blue. Charles had beaten the hell out of him—maybe trying to drown him, and unfortunately, Frank almost deserved it. But the Family took this into hand, had a little meeting, and basically told Mr. Buffington he'd better be out of Colquitt County by sundown.

I lost three more important people in my life in one week in May of 1998: the greatest theatre organist in history, my friend George Wright; the finest popular vocalist in history, Frank Sinatra; and the greatest Auntie Mame a son could ever have, Carolyn.

At Carolyn's funeral many tales were told within the elegance of the First United Methodist Church Sanctuary which exuded Uncle Frank's touch—from organ case to kneeling cushions. One epic that had the congregation howling was a tale I had recounted to the preacher about Carolyn in the early years in Vidalia and how she came to have a certain coldness towards hunting dogs—one of my father's life-long passions. It seems that every time John had to go out of town on business it would rain. And there was Carolyn, feeding the dogs while they literally wrapped their chains around her in the downpour. It's a wonder that she agreed to keep the poodles that Glenn and I had back in the eighties, but Magnolia and Arabella were refined little girls.

My Aunt Susan had met an untimely death in a traffic accident in Moultrie in 1993. And then, on May 19, 1999, just a few days short of the anniversary of Carolyn's death, Aunt Alyce said goodbye. I really couldn't believe it, for just a few months prior, after she had some "heart work" done in Tallahassee, Joan Holman (Moultrie's answer to Sister Woman in *Cat on a Hot Tin Roof*) and I came around to Alyce's that very day for a visit. Alyce was holding her usual court while Sherrod was back in the bedroom dressing for some evening civic function. Alyce asked me to go in the kitchen and fix her a C.C. and Seven, and I exclaimed, "You can't have that!" "Oh yes I can," she assured me, so I obliged and fixed Joan and myself a little cheer as well. We were having a grand time and suddenly Uncle Sherrod emerged in all his glory (he *had* some threads!) and looked over at Alyce, draped in her favorite chair, tinkling the ice cubes in her glass. Sherrod asked, "Why Alyce, what's that in your hand?" "It's just a lil ole' toddy." "Now Alyce, you know you can't have that!" "I *mean*!" she remonstrated. "Muh doctor said I'm fine; *I'm goin' back to all muh ole' ways!*" Sherrod just rolled his eyes, slid open the back door and disappeared in his Mercury. For you uninitiated Yankees, "I mean", in Southern, is our version of your "I mean to tell you."

Now Big A was gone. I got myself together. I was living in Valdosta now after moving Carolyn to a facility there. After her death I continued to live in the house I bought from Berrien Cheatham on High Street. I threw a few things in the car and got ready to go to what I knew would be an endless roundelay of cocktail wakes. When I tried to park on Alice B. Toklas—you guessed it—the only space available was near the *Monsieur's* big gate which protected his *Palazzo* fortress. And Bill Cole was back in residence after a long stay in Coral Gables. We said our hello's and then he took on a very droll visage—one I had never seen before—and said in a very caring tone, "Now John, I know Alyce and I had our differences, but I want you to know that I sho am sorry for you and yo fam'ly." I, taken somewhat aback, said, "Well, Bill that is mighty kind of you; Alyce suffered so these last few weeks; she's in a much better place now." The *Monsieur* walked forward to the gate pickets and said, "But John, are you shuah she's theah?"

I went straight into Sherrod's foyer to recount this latest quip from Mr. Cole. Sherrod just shook with laughter as did Ida Pearl (Alyce bestowed this second name on her, much to her dislike). Cousin Molly did not look very happy and did not laugh. I asked what was wrong and she said, "Johnny, I just can't believe these widah women and the way they're carryin' on 'bout Daddy. We don't even have my momma in the ground good!" Before I could say a thing, Ida got on her soap box and looked at Molly intently. "Molly", Ida said emphatically, "you might as well get ready. Yo Daddy is a guud lookin' man…and those casseroles are gone come rollin' right on i-in!"

After Alyce's death we bravely tried to carry on those wonderful paaaty's and recounted and dredged up all kinds of tales. Like the time Frank went on a Kiwanis trip to Europe with Alyce and a bunch of other fun people. They were to dine in some very fine hotel in Venice with Frank treating. They hadn't even latched onto their menus before Frank said in a low and despondent grunt, "We gone have to leave; they don't take American Express!" Or the time Alyce had a prominent artist paint her portrait. After framing it and hanging it over the pine mantle in the living room she asked Daddy what he thought about it. He responded , "It looks like he did it by telephone." Then, there was my father's close friend, Lamar Moore, who used to tell about their childhood "Sex Club" with the neighborhood girls. (I must not have been as progressive— even decades later—for my club was the "Theatre Organ Club" with Jack Hackett and his tag-along sister Myra Jane!)

And my dear friend, Berrien Cheatham, told a grand one on my cousin, Emily McCall. Emily was the essential spinster complete with a blue hair rinse and a gullibility that almost guaranteed a good story if there was interaction with Berrien after scotch time at 5 p.m. Berrien and Emily were in daily contact, living within earshot of each other in Valdosta. The big news in Lowndes County at the time was the arrival of the new Sam's Wholesale warehouse which was built near I-75. Emily wanted to go, and she couldn't figure out how to get there exactly. She made the mistake of moving from the topic of the price of

Dottie and me chaperoned by Alyce's portrait "done by telephone".
Collection of the Author

asparagus at Harvey's Supermarket and *The New York Times* crossword puzzle to how to find Sam's, and by this time in the discourse, the clock had already insured that the scotch was at the ready on Berrien's end. "Berrien, tell me, how in the world do I get to the new Sam's?" Emily pleaded. "Well it's perfectly easy," Berrien replied between sips of his Dewar's, "just take the *intercourse* down to exit so-and-so and follow the service road."

A few days later, after Emily had been newly rinsed in a lovely shade of Sheffield Blue, she had her bridge club over. Naturally the talk got around to the big news of Sam's in Valdosta and several of the bridge players chimed out together, "How do we get theah?" Emily rared back, pleased as punch that she had the answer and said, "Oh, Berrien says its real easy; you just take the *intercourse*...!" The married element, or at least those who had some sort of *carnival knowledge*, just swooned. Emily was at a complete loss.

I always had fun with an "imported story" told to me by my good friend, Bobby Clark, who grew up in Orangeburg, South Carolina. His father owned a chain of tire stores and Bobby worked there during the summers of his high school years. That was back when the tire store offered gas in addition to Dunlops. One of Orangeburg's finest—we'll just call her Clairese Aikins—drove up one day to Clark Tire Company and Bobby greeted Clairese: "How you doin' Miss Clairese?" "I'm just fine, Bobby," she said as she turned the wheels in her metallic blue Fleetwood so hard that the power steering pump let out a yelp. Bobby continued, "Well, what will it be today?" Mrs. Aikins let her power window down fully—Estee Lauder filling the hot summer air. "Well, let's see...uh, fill it up with Ethyl. Oh, and Herbert said, 'Could you stick your finger in my rear end and see if I need any grease?'" Now this one always sent everybody reeling and popped the toasted pecans right off the cheese wafers!

When Sherrod died, appropriately on July the Fourth, 2005, a certain finality came to bear on the wonderful world I once knew and loved. Sherrod and I actually became very close after Alyce's death; there hadn't been any room on the stage for him as long as Big A was taking the bows. In her last few weeks, I can remember hearing Alyce tell Sherrod, "Now, Sheuud, when I check out, you can see any wumun you wish 'cept for *Marie Bracey*. Marie (always pronounced Maahree, with the emphasis on the first syllable) Bracey, a divoone woman that had much of Alyce's spririt, was a widow from Thomasville, Georgia and had been a sweetheart of Sherrod's before "The Big A Occupation." After Alyce died and a few weeks had passed, he resumed his relationship with Marie and they made a grand and happy couple. I think Alyce had known all along that Sherrod never really got Marie out of his system and after I was around her and in the company of a doting Sherrod, I could certainly see why. She, too, had health issues and died of cancer, leaving Sherrod much alone and certainly not willing to embark on any more relationships. Today, I carefully tend my example of the exquisite pink camellia which has been propagated in her honor.

Sherrod continued to have dinner paaaty's and would ask me to drop by and check out the table. My, you would have thought Uncle Frank had set it—right down to the Chinese Export tureens filled with fresh fruit. People used to say that if someone cancelled a dinner invitation of Frank's at 1177, he would go recruit someone off the street so that the symmetry of the table would be preserved. Sherrod certainly kept the tradition alive. Once a friend, Chris Pippig and I dined with him and we were being attended by Greg Richardson. Greg would come into the dining room, resplendent in his white cutaway, and say, "Did you need me, Mr. Sherrod?" With everything we could want in place, Sherrod would look puzzled and say, "No, Greg, we're fine." In a few minutes this scenario would repeat itself until we finally discovered that Chris had been unknowingly pressing the buzzer (under the Oriental rug) that rang in the kitchen.

Ida would tell about the time she commissioned Uncle Frank to design some new draperies for her Moultrie home. He came by for a cocktail viewing and Ida asked of Frank, "Don't you think they kind uh, kick ouuut, Frank?" "'Coase…they certainly do. I bleeve I'll have a scotch and wawtuh." Actually, Moultrie has always been fond of "viewin's"—which are nothing more than an excuse to get together and drink. My friend, Roger Smith once called me on a spring afternoon and I asked, "What's the occasion?" "We gone have an azalea viewin'," he promised.

I have some other stories to put on the plate as well. A favorite is about my first trip down to see Bill Cole—prior to the time Michael and I pronounced him *the Monsieur*. Bill had become very aware of my intense interest in architecture and the special place I held in my soul for the *Palazzo*. I once even contracted to buy it from him, sold my property in Valdosta, and asked Uncle Sherrod if he thought I was doing the right thing. He said, "Johnny, you're the *only one* that will ever be happy in that house." Bill suddenly had a change of heart and cancelled our agreement. I ended up buying another "Uncle Frank" just down from Tallokas on Crescent Drive. I am writing this epistle from Crescent House at this very moment. And Bill and I remain good friends. But, according to Ida, I should not ever want to speak to the likes of Mr. Cole again…

Bill invited me to travel to Coral Gables and experience the grandeur of his mansion across from the *Venetian Pool*. I had to go. I told him that I was going to come on the *Sunset Limited* and gave him the schedule.

He affirmed that he would arrange to pick me up at the Amtrak station in Miami and that we would drive one of his Cadillacs (yes, he had some of them too) back to Moultrie after my stay in Coral Gables. This sounded perfect to me and Rick Ricks took me to Madison, Florida to catch the *Limited*. Madison doesn't even have a train station, just a shelter with a pay phone. Rick felt a little dubious about leaving me there—nigh to midnight, on the opposite side of the tracks with only my book, *The Future of Architecture* by Frank Lloyd Wright in hand. I sent him home and assured him that I'd be just fine.

Well, the train didn't come and didn't come. I finally called 1-800-USARAIL from the pay phone to see what was going on. *The Limited* was very late and we wouldn't be arriving in Miami until the wee hours. I called Bill to let him know about the change in schedule to which he replied, "Oooo, I'm so glad you called. You know, I forgot to tell you I don't drive at night (he doesn't drive ever!) and you gonna have to get you a taxi to Ca'rl Gables; and get one that speaks English." I was livid!

When I finally de-trained in Miami there were only two cabbies and it was hard choosing which of the two exhibited the lighter side of the Cuban language! I don't actually think that anyone ever goes to Coral Gables from the Miami Amtrak Station. The balance of the early morning was spent going to everywhere *but* Coral Gables, with many an intercession to ask police for directions. At dawn, we finally were on De Soto and I found myself crawling though palm hedges and Brinks Security signs to try and find Bill's place. I finally found the house— which was something to behold—and I was promptly put on a roll-away bed in his conservatory with statues of the four seasons watching carefully over me from above. I slept well and finally got up and found him in the kitchen watching a miniscule TV and drinking un-refrigerated "Co-Cola". I waited to be offered something for breakfast but nothing was forthcoming. I finally said, "Bill, do you happen to have something I could put in my tummy so I can take these pills?" "Let's see, well I've got some popcorn," sounding like a boy scout that got his Eagle pin. I said, "Perhaps something else?" "Oh, I know," said Bill pridefully; "you can go pick you a grapefruit outside." Which I promptly did. Back in the kitchen, I stood there with the grapefruit in hand but no bowl or utensils were forthcoming either. "Bill, do you have something I could use to maybe cut this?" "Heah, sugah," he beamed, "here's a knife." It was a plastic serrated one from McDonald's still in its hermetically sealed plastic wrapper.

We actually had a good time on my visit and since Bill eats every meal out, I did get some decent food at the Piccadilly Cafeteria and some Chinese restaurant that offered a Lobster Special. The next day, I began to pack one of Bill's various and sundry Cadillacs for the trip back to Moultrie. We had already taken Bill's dogs to the vet and it was time to hit the road.

In the midst of my wrestling with some steamer trunk of his, the *Monsieur* came out to the porte cochere with his arms firmly anchored at each side of his waist. Looking to the sky above he pronounced, "Sugah, it's just not in the stars for me to travel today."

I couldn't believe what I was hearing. I lashed out and I said, "Bill I *have* to be back in Moultrie tomorrow; I work for a living and I've got client appointments plus my mother has already given me a guilt trip about leaving her at The Colquitt this weekend." "Well, I'm so sorry, but it's just not in the stars." I was ready to show him some stars. "What do you propose that I do?" "I guess you'll have to take the train," he said as he clasped his hands. "The train runs every other day, Bill," I yelled back. "Well," he offered, "I guess you'll have to fly back." *And rent a car from Tallahassee to Moultrie? Hell no!* "Ohh, he suddenly gushed, I know, I know!" We went to the kitchen and he pulled out a utensil drawer and handed me an old cash register receipt on which he had scribbled some times. "That's the bus schedule to Moultrie from Miamuh (that's the way Dottie Wright always pronounced it)." "The **bus** schedule?", I wailed. "Yeah, and you'll have to call a cab 'cause I can't drive you theah."

I was smoldering but I had no choice. The Miami bus station was a revelation. I had to literally walk over people lying on the dirty floor; I was the only South Georgia boy in captivity. The bus trip was long and arduous; we had a layover in Tallahassee, then in the late afternoon the next day, we finally rolled into Moultrie. The bus station was just a few blocks from The Colquitt. I rounded up my luggage and my two-day beard and popped into Carolyn's room on the first floor. "Well, did you have a good time, sweetie?" Carolyn asked. "Oh yes, it was just grand." I promptly went upstairs, unplugged the phone, and slept for what seemed to be a fortnight.

Michael Kelly and I were to go visit Bill again as you know. The only reason I dredge this up is that every time I tell the story about my first trip to Coral Gables, Ida says tearfully, "My Laud, and he wuz foolish enuff to go back ag'in!"

Moultrie isn't the drinking town it used to be so there isn't any juicy paaaty material to tell anymore. Even though the great opera singer James Melton was born here, the biggest festival we have is a car show and an agricultural exposition. My interior design practice was never dependent on Moultrie, thank the Lord, 'cause Uncle Frank had spent 'em dry prior to my arrival.

The *Palazzo* continues to be lovingly cared for by *the Monsieur* but the only activity passing through those crested gates is for some

My partner, Mitch Parker arriving at the *Palazzo* to chauffeur *Monsieur Cole*.
Collection of the Author

refurbishing project, or the lawn man, or my life partner, Mitch and I picking Bill up for a trip to eat in nearby Thomasville. For a while, Mitch and I owned Bill's Continental Mark II but we let it go to a gentleman who had the resources to restore it as one of the finest examples of the marque, produced only in 1956-57.There are still a few in Moultrie and environs who can recall tales such as those I've told like the late Lamar Moore, or Cooka Hillebrand, Bennett Willis, Berrien Cheatham, Ida Murphy, my Aunt Sarah Tharpe, and our dear friend, Mimi Platter— perhaps the most gracious and elegant lady that ever adorned Moultrie. But, in putting this all down on paper, I realize now the finality that follows this Southern epic. I really wasn't sure that what I had was publishable, since it was all *true*. I have always maintained that if "the book took", then Mitch and I might best move to Switzerland.

I guess that's why I have never owned many books of fiction. Once upon a time, in Moultrie, the real was *surreal*—very much like the *Palazzo* that towers above all the other Frank McCall houses on Alice B. Toklas. Once you reach Allegood's Grocery, you are out of "the histerical district" and back to an everyday reality where…

"They—riding arm-in-arm, leave their trash to the fading town and head back to the farm."

LaVergne, TN USA
04 April 2011
222759LV00002B/1/P